JAPAN'S
INTRACTABLE
PROBLEMS
AND
AMERICAN
INVOLVEMENT

JAPAN'S INTRACTABLE PROBLEMS AND AMERICAN INVOLVEMENT

MINORU YANAGIHASHI

ARPress
ILLUMINATING IDEAS
EMPOWERING VOICES

ARPress
45 Dan Road Suite 5
Canton MA 02021

Hotline:	1(888) 821-0229
Fax:	1(508) 545-7580

Ordering Information:

Quantity sales. Special discounts are available on quantity purchases by corporations, associations, and others. For details, contact the publisher at the address above.

Printed in the United States of America.

ISBN-13:	Softcover	979-8-89356-920-9
	eBook	979-8-89356-921-6

Library of Congress Control Number: 2024905790

CONTENTS

PART I: CONSTITUTIONAL REVISION

PART II: TERRITORIAL DISPUTES

PREFACE

When a nation's constitution has not been revised or any corrections made for over seventy-five years, and its dispute with neighboring countries over small islands have not been resolved for the same length of time, they present serious problems for Japanese political leaders. The challenges, with their stress and strain, have consumed an inordinate amount of the leadership's attention. In all these problems, a foreign country is involved—the United States.

For the average Japanese, constitutional issues and territorial quarrels over small islands are not uppermost in their thinking. They worry about bread-and-butter issues, or to say it colloquially, rice and soy sauce issues. Socioeconomic problems such as the cost of living and the aging population are of pressing concern. To be sure, these are challenging problems affecting day-to-day living.

However, from a long-term perspective, the constitutional and island sovereignty issues have serious implications for Japan's future. They began to raise questions among many Japanese. In the late 1960s and into the 1970s, the Japanese asked themselves some basic questions—what does it mean to be Japanese? Where is Japan headed? What is Japan's proper place in the world? A proliferation of publications discussed these and other related questions. A broad cross-section of the population, including writers, journalists, artists, academics, and government officials participated. This phenomenon is known as *Nihonjinron* ("Japanese theory" or "theories about the Japanese"). Discussions covered a wide range of subject areas, including history, society, customs, arts, science, architecture, literature, philosophy, psychology, politics, and economics. *Nihonjinron* is more than a search for self-identity or cultural identity; it is a search for national identity.

Why would the Japanese be concerned with national and self-introspection? After the catastrophic defeat in a war, Japan in the 1960s and 1970s was in a period of double-digit economic growth. Such growth was a surprise and was called an "economic miracle." Japanese did not become suddenly affluent, far from it, but rapid growth brought about huge transformations in society and culture—dramatically affecting lifestyle and the environment. Moreover, there was an anomaly. An emergent economic superpower was simultaneously a dwarf political actor dependent on the United States. During the Occupation of Japan, the US exercised commanding power, but this domineering influence continued even after the Occupation. Japan could not defend itself militarily and politically had to follow the lead of the United States. This subservience, plus the rapid changes domestically and internationally, brought on uncertainty, insecurity, restlessness, and doubt. People began to ask questions.

Among the myriads of possible questions in this book, I am concerned with the political questions—what is the nature of the Japanese nation-state, and in what direction is it headed? Two constitutional issues were selected: the status of the emperor, and Article 9 with its "war renunciation clause." They were chosen because they relate to the questions posed above. Most observers would agree these two constitutional issues are the most controversial. Likewise, I have selected the territorial disputes, as they pertain to the question of Japan's direction and are bound up with Article 9. Article 9 is involved because some perception of coercive force may be necessary to support diplomatic actions to resolve island disputes. Therefore, two sets of controversies—the emperor's status/Article 9 and the island disputes—are the subject matter of this book. As Japan emerged from the devastation of the war, it confronted these two sets of issues. First the question of constitutional reform and soon afterwards, a series of territorial disputes over small islands. Even though Japan coalesced, became a stable and democratic society, and soon developed the third-largest economy in the world, these controversies plagued domestic politics and affected its relationship with neighboring countries. And the issues have persisted.

The two sets of problems have long-term implications. They are intertwined and determine what role Japan plays as a purported world leader. Does it want to be a bold assertive nation or a passive pacific-leaning nation? Does it continue as a junior partner in its alliance with the US, or does it take a more independent approach? How unified could Japan be as it carries out its stated objectives? These two sets of problems, therefore, are of considerable interest.

To understand how these intractable issues arose, it is necessary to go back to their historical roots. Potentially sensitive issues are usually discussed and debated far in advance by policy planners. The study takes a look at the planning process. There are records of discussions in the form of position papers, proposals, and recommendations. However, the decisions made by policy planners may not be the final word or may not be carried out. Indeed, implementation can be problematic. New factors or events can intervene, and decisions can be affected by the whims of policymakers. Even so, the role of planning is important, for it sets the tone and direction and provides the basis for further discussions. The importance of planning should not be minimized.

Part I deals with constitutional revision and begins with a chapter on preplanning and pre-surrender or wartime planning and the problem of the status of the Japanese emperor. It is followed by a chapter on the drafting of Article 9 with its "renunciation of war" clause. To see how these highly controversial clauses became part of the Constitution of Japan requires going back to the American planners who discussed these issues during the war. The declassification of documents in the 1970s allowed for a reassessment of the roles played by the American participants. The origins of the controversial clauses may be difficult to ascertain because they may have evolved from discussions that are not in the reports. But the interpretations of the provisions are clear-cut. The major changes in the interpretation can be traced from its beginning to the present time. The so-called "reinterpretation" of Article 9 is striking and reveals how realpolitik can change a clause to fit the needs of the country—to shift from non-participation to active self-defense. In the planning, discussions and negotiations, the role played by key individuals is highlighted. Their views and personalities had an impact on the final policy or document outcome. Part I ends with a chapter on the movements for constitutional reform. Immediately after the promulgation of the 1947 Constitution, there were flurries of discussions and debates over the document. Some wanted specific and technical changes, while others wanted a complete overhaul. The majority of the public favored the Constitution and were against any revision. After Japan regained its sovereignty, revisionist movements arose in earnest and became emotional and ideological. A revision of the constitution became one of the main platforms of the dominant Liberal Democratic Party (LDP). Different drafts of the constitution drawn up by the LDP will be explored and the reasons why they failed to be implemented. The chapter ends with a discussion of the prospects for reform.

Part II is concerned with the small island disputes. Japan is made up of four main islands, Hokkaido, Honshu, Shikoku, and Kyushu, which are large enough to support population centers, extensive agricultural acreage, and a spread of industrial facilities and supporting infrastructures. The four principal islands are referred to as Japan proper or mainland Japan. Surrounding Japan proper are close to seven thousand small islands, but the majority are uninhabited. Many are massive volcanic rocks jutting out of the ocean and are called islets. Japan claims sovereignty over all these islands and islets, and there are no challenges to the claims because they are close enough to be within the recognized territorial jurisdiction of Japan.

Wartime policy planners ignored or paid little attention to these small islands because they were considered insignificant. The planners had no way of predicting how events or trends would make a few of these islands controversial. However, toward the end of the war, the importance of these islands began to be recognized and considered in postwar negotiations and agreements. At this point, they became centers of disputes.

When a nation makes a claim of territorial sovereignty over a group of islands and it is challenged by a neighboring country, the ensuing arguments are couched in the language of the United Nations Convention on the Law of the Sea (UNCLOS). The terms and concepts codified in UNCLOS are used by nations in their claims and counterclaims. To understand the arguments, it is necessary to define and illustrate how these terms and concepts are used. Chapter 4 covers the terminology of UNCLOS, the points of controversy, and the wartime planning and major power conferences where early negotiations and settlements took place.

Chapter 5 focuses on the three major territorial disputes, Kuril Islands or Northern Territories, Dokdo Islands or Takeshima, and Senkaku Islands or Diaoyutai. Each country has its own name for the islands. For example, the islets between mainland Korea and Japan in the Sea of Japan are known as Dokdo in Korean and Takeshima in Japanese.

In this book, each major island dispute has a subheading. Under the subheading, the origin of the dispute and its development over the years are covered. The territorial dispute may wax and wane over a period of time. It may suddenly erupt because a foreign naval vessel or fishing boat was intruding into claimed territorial waters, or it could be a foreign plane flying into the claimed air space over the islands. It could be a high-level foreign leader visiting the site or making provocative statements. These so-called provocations could lead to immediate pushback with accusations and threats and even mass protests by citizens. After a few weeks, it dies down and is put on the back burner. But the problem is not solved.

The final chapter (chapter 6) discusses the implications of how the emperor is viewed and how the conservative stance has changed. The role of nationalism and the rise of militarism are linked historically to the imperial institution. But today, nationalistic and militaristic motivations play a more vital part in the small island disputes. The Kuril Islands started as the first territorial dispute, and presently, it is stalemated. Ominously, there are signs of increasing militarization on the part of the Russians. Dokdo has become an emotional issue, especially for South Koreans, but the possibility of open conflict is quite remote. The most dangerous is the Senkaku Islands. It is the last of the territorial quarrels to emerge but is potentially a source of conflict between China and Japan. The US has a defense alliance with Japan and would be drawn into the conflict. Of the three disputes, the strategic importance of the Senkaku Island for Japan and China places it on a different tier.

Strategic analysts point to the location of the Senkaku Islands and Dokdo. They are in the midst of a busy sea transit lane that makes them important, especially in the case of the Senkakus, which is in the passage lane used by many countries, including the United States. A major reason for their importance is the actual and potential rich resources in the waters around these islands. The fishing resources are quite abundant around the Kurils and the Senkakus. For the long-term, there are other valuable resources at stake, such as gas, oil, and mineral deposits in the seabed surrounding the islands. These are tangible values, but probably more important is the symbolic value of national prestige. No country wants to lose their claimed territory. Nations are willing to fight over every piece of land. It is a matter of national honor.

The book is intended for the general audience. Government proceedings tend to be complex with a labyrinth of committees and organizations. I have not included every twist and turn of the proceedings, nor is it necessary to go into extensive details. It would only complicate an already obtuse process. Territorial disputes have terminological challenges. Sovereignty claims to territory are couched in terms of "zones." These "zones" are measured from the coastline extending out into the sea and the whole area is under the jurisdiction of the coastal state. The distances are standardized by the United Nations Convention on the Law of the Sea. But some of these terms are defined in several ways and governments have their choice of preferred definition. This results in a wide range of interpretations and introduces ambiguity. The use of acronyms is common in governmental operations. A list of abbreviations is provided to help decipher these acronyms. Acronyms are commonly used to denote political parties. In addition, commentators often use the Japanese name for the political party. A troublesome example is the small Japanese political party, the *Nippon Ishin no Kai,* which is sometimes shortened to *"Nippon Ishin."* It is translated as the Japan Innovation Party with the acronym JIP or as the Japan Restoration Party with the acronym JRP. Regardless of the linguistic challenges, the aim is to make the narrative understandable for the reader. The macron, a diacritical mark placed above a vowel has been omitted from Japanese words. Footnotes are provided for those seeking further information. Additional references are listed for the specialists and those wanting extensive background information.

ACKNOWLEDGMENTS

Two academics, who are now deceased, influenced my thoughts on the subjects covered in the book. Professor Robert E. Ward, my mentor at the University of Michigan, enlightened me on the complexities of constitutional reforms. He taught and retired from Stanford University. Professor Pilkyu Kim, my former graduate student at the University of Arizona, rekindled my interest in small island disputes. He went on to teach and retire from the University of Maryland.

On the home front, Mark, my son, assisted with the digital aspects of the manuscript. Lisa, my daughter, edited the manuscript and made the text more readable. My partner, Evelyn, endured the extended period it took to complete the project.

ABBREVIATIONS

ADIZ   air defense identification zone
ASDF   Air Self-Defense Force
CAC   Country and Area Committee
CDP   Constitutional Democratic Party
CGL   Coast Guard Law
CGP   Clean Government Party
DPJ   Democratic Party of Japan
DPP   Democratic Party for the People
DSR   Division of Special Service
EEZ   exclusive economic zone
FEC   Far Eastern Commission
GDP   gross domestic product
GSDF   Ground Self-Defense Force
ICJ   International Court of Justice
JCP   Japan Communist Party
JIP   Japan Innovation Party

or

JRP   Japan Restoration Party
JSP   Japan Socialist Party
LDP   Liberal Democratic Party
MSDF   Maritime Self-Defense Force
NDPG   National Defense Program Guidelines

NPR	National Police Reserve
NSC	National Security Council
NSF	National Safety Force
PAP	People's Armed Police
PKO	Peacekeeping Operations
PLA	People's Liberation Army
PRC	People's Republic of China
PWC	Postwar Programs Committee
ROC	Republic of China (Taiwan)
ROK	Republic of Korea (South Korea)
SCAP	Supreme Commander for the Allied Powers
SCAPIN	SCAP Instructions (or Index Number)
SDF	Self-Defense Force
SFE	Subcommittee for the Far East
SIPRI	Stockholm International Peace Research Institute
SWNCC	State-War-Navy Coordinating Committee
UNCLOS	United Nations Convention on the Law of the Sea
UNPKO	United Nations Peacekeeping Operations
USSR	Union of Soviet Socialist Republic

PART I

CONSTITUTIONAL REVISION

PLANNING AND THE STATUS OF THE EMPEROR

CHAPTER ONE

The Japanese Constitution is a remarkable and unique document. It was promulgated on November 3, 1946, and became effective on May 3, 1947. It has not been amended or revised and is, therefore, the oldest unamended constitution in the world. Considered to be one of the most democratic constitutions ever designed, it includes civil rights that are not even in the US Constitution. The Constitution of Japan renounces the use of war as a sovereign right and prohibits threat or force to settle international disputes. There is no other nation that has explicitly rejected the use of military force as a policy instrument. How could such a progressive and pacifist constitution come about?

At the beginning of the twentieth century, Japan emerged as a military power in Asia after defeating China in the Sino-Japanese War of 1894-95 and Russia in the Russo-Japanese War of 1904-05. The United States started to view Japan as a major threat to its role in Asia and throughout the Pacific region. Relations between the countries continued to deteriorate, and by the late 1930s, the military of both countries began to plan for possible armed conflict. In the political realm, American officials started to make contingency plans on how to handle a defeated Japan, assuming, of course, a US military victory.

American planners learned the importance of preplanning from the experience of World War I. There was no preparation on what to do with Germany after the surrender. Germany was treated harshly at the Versailles Conference, and the Weimar Republic, established to govern the country, was structurally weak and beset with economic problems. It was left in a weakened condition and an opening was created for authoritarian control. By the mid-1920s, the Nazis had taken control. Perhaps, preplanning could have avoided the devastating outcome.

Preplanning was undertaken by the Department of State almost a year before the Pearl Harbor attack. It is surprising how early contingency planning began on how to address a defeated enemy; it was hypothetical planning. On February 3, 1941, the State Department started the prewar planning by secretly forming the Division of Special Research (DSR). It was headed by Dr. Leo Pasvolsky, Special Assistant to Secretary of State Cordell Hall. He was an economist and had worked in various capacities in the State Department. Assisting Pasvolsky were Charles W. Yost, the diplomat, and Harley Notter, a career State Department official. The DSR was charged with preparing reports of possible problems arising in the postwar period. Much of the discussions in the meetings revolved around broad principles covering the occupation of the defeated country. It was also responsible for broadening the scope of its work by making subcommittee assignments. The DSR had met for only a few sessions when the Pearl Harbor attack occurred, and soon afterwards, the DSR was disbanded.

Immediately after Pearl Harbor, the State Department decided to expand the planning process. At this point, the Allies were on the defensive and the news from the front line was bleak. The tide of the battle did not turn in America's favor until the defeat of the Japanese Imperial Navy at Midway in June of 1942. With the Guadalcanal campaign (August 7, 1942 - February 9, 1943), the US went on the offensive. During the entire period of wartime planning, intense combat continued unabated. However, the planners assumed victory was assured, and the policies under discussion would be needed in occupied Japan and Germany.

The State Department took the initiative and made it a showcase of planning. It is surprising how their efforts were so careful and detailed. At this time, there was almost no input from the military or other agencies. There was no need to consult and coordinate with other entities. This allowed for the occupation policies of Japan to be more cohesive than those of Germany. The indirect approach was used in Japan, allowing the Japanese government to implement and administer the policies, whereas in Germany, the direct approach was used with the US military government in charge of all phases.

The expansion of the planning process began with the establishment of an umbrella organization, the Advisory Committee on Postwar Foreign Policy. This advisory committee was tasked with preparing recommendations for President Franklin D. Roosevelt on post-World War II foreign policy. It held its first meeting on February 12, 1942, two months after Pearl Harbor. Dr. George H. Blakeslee, Professor of History and International Relations at Clark University, led the committee, and Yost served as an assistant, while Notter was a member. Blakeslee opened the meeting by asking a pointed question, "Assuming that we win the war, what are the principles upon which we would base any peace to be enforced on Japan?"[1]

Dr. George H. Blakeslee
Courtesy of Wikipedia

Five subcommittees and three special subcommittees were created under the advisory committee. Three of the subcommittees dealt with political matters: Political Problems Subcommittee, Territorial Problems

---

1. Hugh Borton, *Spanning Japan's Modern Century: The Memoirs of Hugh Borton* (Lanham, MD: Lexington Books, 2002), 80.

Subcommittee, and Security Problems Subcommittee. These three subcommittees formulated reports and proposals on specific questions and transmitted them to the Advisory Committee on Postwar Foreign Policy, which then forwarded the documents to President Roosevelt and his staff. Since these three subcommittees addressed political issues, they are our concern in this book. Of the three subcommittees, the most important for our discussion is the Territorial Problems Subcommittee. It was staffed by several Japanese specialists and was given the task of handling territorial disputes and settlements in such problem areas as the Japanese Mandated Islands, Okinawa, Kurils, and Southern Sakhalin.[2] The other two subcommittees dealt with economic issues and are outside the scope of this book. The subcommittees turned out to be the key planning bodies where decisions and recommendations were made. The Secretary of State Hall had a penchant for forming committees, and for a while, there was a constant fluctuation of committees. He finally concluded that he preferred relying on the smaller subcommittees to the larger committees.

A notable feature of the early planning was the quality of the personnel handling the Japanese questions. Forty-five committee members came from outside the government. They included academics who taught Japanese history, politics and culture, businessmen, and individuals from organizations associated with Japan. Government officials included senators, congressmen, low-ranking and middle-echelon foreign service officers from the State Department, White House staff members, and a specialist from the Library of Congress.

There were eight individuals who had in-depth knowledge about Japan. They were from academia or were diplomats with extended experience in Japan. These individuals were characterized as Japan experts, but their language skills varied, with the younger members more proficient with the language. Among the academics, the younger Dr. Hugh Borton had mastered the Japanese language while the older scholars, such as Dr. Blakeslee, were not versed in Japanese, although they taught courses on Asia and Japan at the university. In those days, few were proficient in Japanese, partly because there was a paucity of schools offering Japanese studies in America. It necessitated enrolling

---

2. Borton, *Spanning*, 93.

in a Japanese or a European university to have any specialization in Japanese studies.[3]

The character of the policy-planning group and the personalities of its members are important factors to consider when evaluating performance. The majority of the members of the advisory committee and its subcommittees embodied the values of liberal idealism. Many were highly educated, and several were associated with Ivy League colleges, the hotbed of liberalism. They favored a non-punitive approach and did not want to severely weaken Japan. There was a danger in drastically stripping Japan, as it could lead to social and political instability and economic dislocation and would prevent the development of democratic institutions and practices.

Some planners did not trust the Japanese. They thought the Japanese may accept democratic reforms at the beginning, but it was questionable whether they would continue to embrace these reforms. Stanley Hornbeck, a career diplomat and advisor to Hull, believed Japan should be isolated and suppressed indefinitely to ensure the acceptance of democratic practices. Such ideas were strongly opposed by the liberal majority, who insisted there was no need for long-term suppression.

A small minority believed in a harsher approach with Japan being stripped of almost everything. They felt the committee was being too lenient towards Japan, but they lacked a leader with the stature and forcefulness of Henry Morgenthau, who was an advocate for a stern approach to the occupation of Germany.Morgenthau, the Secretary of the Treasury, wanted Germany to be reduced to an agricultural state, stripped of heavy industries. Initially, Roosevelt went along with the Morgenthau Plan, but he was soon dissuaded to move away from the plan by Secretary of War Henry Stimson and by Secretary of State Cordell Hull. Morgenthau advised the committee to follow the harsh policy used in Germany. The majority of the planners thought otherwise and ignored his recommendation.

---

3. Rudolf V.A. Janssens, *What Future for Japan? U.S. Wartime Planning for the Postwar Era, 1942-1945* (Amsterdam: Rodopi, 1995), 77.

By the beginning of 1944, the Advisory Committee on Postwar Foreign Policy was restructured into a more refined policy-planning body. Changes were made in the committee system with the termination of the subcommittees and the transfer of work to a new committee, the Postwar Programs Committee (PWC).

The Advisory Committee, which held only four sessions, was finally terminated and replaced by the PWC on January 15, 1944. The PWC was formed to address the need for long-range postwar planning and was geared to formulate specific policy directives. Since it was in the upper echelon of the Department of State, it was designed for top-level planners.

The PWC lasted about a year, and in the final wartime policy committee change, it was replaced by the State-War-Navy Coordinating Committee (SWNCC). SWNCC met for the first time on December 19, 1944. It was formed to anticipate the political and military issues that could arise in the occupation of Germany and Japan following the end of the war. For the first time, an integrated committee of civilian and military planners was established. The early efforts of SWNCC were concentrated on Germany. When the attention shifted to Japan, the subunit concerned with Japan was the Subcommittee for the Far East (SFE), chaired by Eugene H. Dooman. Dooman was a diplomat, fluent in Japanese, who for many years was with the US Embassy in Tokyo. The SFE became the primary planning committee, preparing many directives, several of which became basic policy guidelines for the Occupation[4]. SWNCC was the forerunner of what is today the US National Security Council, the top advisory body on foreign policy and security matters. SWNCC was the first attempt to coordinate the resources of the Pentagon and the State Department, combining military and civilian specialists in comprehensive policymaking. The format used by SWNCC was to have a number of working groups, each assigned specific problems, and to have their findings presented to the committee.

With the development of PWC and SWNCC, the influence of the core planners, the "Japan crowd" specialists, diminished

---

4. Department of State. *Postwar Foreign Policy Preparation, 1939-1945* (Washington, DC: Government Printing Office, 1949), 67-213.

as administration and defense officials were brought in and more coordination was required. The term "Japan crowd" was used to differentiate the Japan specialists from those specializing in China in the State Department. One can say that by 1944, the role of the core planners or "Japan crowd" had considerably lessened. Nevertheless, several core planners continued to hold key positions in the committees, and a strong consensus of views prevailed among them.

The demise of the "Japan crowd" in the State Department became evident at the beginning of the Truman administration. Joseph C. Grew, the undersecretary of state, was replaced by Dean Acheson. Grew was ambassador to Japan from 1931 to 1941 and was the most visible and long-term pro-Japan advocate in the department. Further evidence of the change was the appointment of George Atcheson, Jr., a China specialist, as advisor to General MacArthur. Two established Japan specialist in the department, Eugene Dooman and Joseph Ballantine, were bypassed. Only a few Japan specialists were left, including Dr. Borton, who stayed with the department until 1948. Besides the shift in the orientation of the State Department, another change to be noted was the move from Washington to Tokyo for most of the planning and implementation of occupation policies. The policies became the responsibility of MacArthur and his staff in Tokyo.

STATUS OF THE EMPEROR

Of all the issues confronting the American occupiers, the most vexing and controversial was the question of what to do with the emperor. The Allied Occupation had two major objectives—demilitarization and democratization.[5] The problem of the emperor was a critical part of the democratization of Japan, and the success in achieving this objective was dependent on how the emperor was handled.

It was obvious from the beginning that drastic changes had to be made to have the Meiji Constitution of 1889 conform to the objectives of the Occupation. Chapter 1 of the Meiji Constitution pertains to

---

5. The official title is the Allied Occupation of Japan, but in reality, it could be called an American Occupation of Japan.

the emperor, and of its seventeen articles, the first four are of prime importance. They are as follows:

Article 1. The Empire of Japan shall be reigned over and governed by a line of Emperors unbroken for ages eternal.

Article 2. The Imperial Throne shall be succeeded to by Imperial male descendants, according to the provisions of the Imperial House Law.

Article 3. The emperor is sacred and inviolable.

Article 4. The emperor is the head of the Empire, combining in Himself the rights of sovereignty, and exercise them, according to the provisions of the present Constitution.[6]

When viewed from a democratic perspective, there were serious flaws in the 1889 Constitution. Sovereignty did not lie with the people. Supreme authority was given to the emperor, who was "divine." The relationship between the major institutions of government was ambiguous and led to conflicts between various entities, resulting in several crises. The cabinet was not mentioned, and neither was a body of elderly elites who made important decisions. The army and navy ministers in the cabinet had to be active-duty officers, which gave the military enormous influence; they could dissolve the cabinet. The loose provisions of the constitution allowed for the military, ultra-nationalistic organizations, and elite groups to usurp the emperor's authority, thereby legitimizing their actions.

Discussions about the emperor and the imperial institution began seriously in early 1943. It first appeared in a paper of the Subcommittee on Political Problems, dated March 10th. The retention of the emperor and the Imperial Household Ministry is listed as one of a series of major issues to be discussed.[7] It was followed on May 25, 1943, by

---

6. Hirobumi Ito, *Commentaries on the Constitution of the Empire of Japan*. Translated by Miyoji Ito, 3rd ed. (Tokyo: Chu-o Daigaku, 1931).

7. National Archives, Diplomatic Section, Notter Files, Box 57, P-213. The information in this section is based on the documents from the Notter Files in the National Archives. The files are named after Harley A. Notter, Executive Secretary of the Advisory Committee on

the first formal paper on the status of the emperor, which provided background information and laid out the policy options available. Arguments are provided for either terminating the imperial institution or continuing it.[8] No preference is stated in the paper, but the case for continuation is more detailed and persuasively presented. It was widely known that the majority of the planners were in favor of continuing the emperorship. Those supporting the retention of the emperor and the imperial institution were the "Japan crowd," including advisers such as Hugh Borton, George H. Blakeslee, Robert A. Fearey, Joseph C. Grew, Eugene H. Dooman, and Joseph Ballantine. Opposition came from the "China crowd," which included Dean Acheson and Owen Lattimore, a noted China scholar. In the committees, the "Japan crowd" and the "China crowd" were grouped together. On certain topics such as the emperorship, there were heated discussions between the groups. In their criticism of the imperial system, the "China crowd" led by Acheson insisted on the abdication of the emperor.

Four months later, they were still discussing the retention of the emperor.In a September 27, 1943, paper, the argument was made that if the emperor is maintained, then the retention of the emperor should be mentioned in the surrender instrument for Japan. This argument became a point of controversy during the drafting of the Potsdam Declaration toward the end of the war, seeking the unconditional surrender of Japan. On October 6, 1943, Dr. Hugh Borton presented an extraordinary paper entitled: "Japan: Postwar Political Problems," in which he pointed out the need for constitutional change. Borton served three years as a Quaker missionary in Japan and studied Japanese history at Columbia University and Leyden University in the Netherlands. In his paper, Borton argued for political changes but maintaining the emperor system with certain limitations, "It is one of the most permanent aspects of postwar political Japan. As such, it may be a valuable factor in the establishment of a stable and moderate postwar government." He believed the political changes should not be imposed by the Occupation but should be made by the Japanese

---

Postwar Foreign Policy. He participated in the operation of various subcommittees. The files were declassified in 1974. The records reveal the thinking of American officials in their discussions.

8. Notter Files, Box 63, T-315, May 25, 1943. "Status of the Japanese Emperor."

themselves.[9] The impact of the principles laid out by Borton can be seen in the SWNCC papers of November and December 1945. These principles provided the rationale for the provisions in the SWNCC documents, which became the guidelines for the American occupiers.

Dr. Hugh Borton

Courtesy of Digital Museum of the History of Japanese in NY

There were other reports on the emperor system, but an exceptional seminal report was presented by Borton on February 23, 1944. It describes the pros and cons of retaining or eliminating the imperial institution and adopting a policy of refraining from criticizing the emperor and the imperial institution.[10] It was clear to Borton why the emperor system had to be supported. Few Americans have Japanese language skills, and a large number of individuals would be needed to govern the country. By retaining the imperial system, it would make it easier for the American occupiers. The emperor would remain, but his functions would be suspended. Since the Japanese have deep reverence for the emperor, any attempt to dissuade them would create a chaotic

---

9. Notter Files, Box 65, T-381, October 6, 1943. "Japan: Postwar Political Problems." Dr. Borton taught modern Japanese history at Columbia University and was later president of Haverford College. He was with the State Department from 1942 to 1948.

10. Notter Files, H-114a.

situation. In the future, if necessary, the emperor could be dethroned if the people no longer felt loyal to the emperor.[11]

The planners favored the retention of the emperorship; it would expedite the surrender and help establish a stable and acceptable Japanese government. The forceful elimination of the imperial institution would be unworkable and against American interests. Therefore, by the beginning of 1944, the planners recommended the emperor and the imperial institution be retained and supported.

At the next level, which was the highest level in the State Department, the planning papers were of two types—Country and Area Committees (CAC) papers and Postwar Programs Committee (PWC) papers. This series of papers began to appear in 1944, focusing on what operational steps could be taken. They covered the possible use and reform of the imperial institution, the supervision of imperial functions, possible abdication of the emperor, relocation of residence, treatment of imperial property, access and security for the emperor and family, and how the emperor as a symbol that could be used for good or evil. Furthermore, the use of the emperor for surrender purposes was discussed.[12] When compared to the planning papers of 1943-1944, the PWC papers were more specific and operational. They were ready to be implemented.

A CAC paper of July 1944 outlined the distinction between Hirohito the reigning emperor, and the imperial institution. Should the military government seek the deposition of Hirohito while recognizing the institution of the emperor? The recommendation was that it should not do this and cited international law as the main reason. Moreover, it asked whether the United Nations should attempt to have Hirohito abdicate the throne. Reasons were given why this move would be useful, but in the end, the recommendation was that the military government should refrain from any actions designed to bring about the emperor's abdication.

---

11. Hugh Borton, *American Presurrender Planning for Postwar Japan* (New York: East Asian Institute, Columbia University, 1967), 15-16.

12. Robert E. Ward, "Presurrender Planning: Treatment of the Emperor and Constitutional Change," in *Democratizing Japan: The Allied Occupation*, ed. Robert E. Ward and Yoshikazu Sakamoto (Honolulu: University of Hawai'i Press, 1987), 6-7.

The next step for the policies devised by the PWC and the CAC of the State Department was to have the proposals accepted and adopted as official policies of the United States government. The approval had to go beyond the State Department. Since the military would be implementing the occupation policies, the War and Navy departments would have to approve. Thus, the proposals were forwarded to the civilian and military planners of SWNCC.

After the initial meeting of SWNCC in December 1944, starting on January 5, 1945, Borton and other Japan specialists in the Subcommittee for the Far East (SFE) began to prepare SWNCC policy papers. Of interest are two papers written by Borton pertaining to the emperor—"The Treatment of the Person of the Emperor" (SWNCC-55) and "The Treatment of the Institution of the Emperor" (SWNCC-209). Here again, the distinction is made between the person of the emperor and the imperial institution. In both papers, the views advanced by Borton, and other Japan specialists remained consistent. The Emperor and the imperial institution should be retained. They did not believe the emperor or the imperial system was the cause of Japan's prewar ultranationalism and military expansionism. The emperor would be under the authority of the American occupation force, so there would be no problem with usurpation of authority. The emperor could be removed, but this should be done by the Japanese people. If the emperor is tried as a war criminal, the task of the Occupation would become more difficult.[13]

The question of what to do with the emperor continued to be troublesome after Germany surrendered and the Pacific War was coming to an end. State Department planners worked on a draft of the Potsdam Declaration with some input from British officials, but it was drafted primarily in the Pentagon. The declaration would impose the requirements for the unconditional surrender of Japan, and with the acceptance of the terms, the war would end. An early draft of the declaration contained a provision for the retention of the emperor and the imperial institution if it was suitably reformed. But the drafters decided to delete it completely. When the declaration was given on July 26, 1945, it had no mention of the emperor. Some said the US

---

13. Borton, *Spanning*, 148-49.

government purposely kept the status of the emperor ambiguous, thus giving the Allies greater flexibility as occupiers. Most historians would say the American planners could not agree on the exact wording; therefore, the question about the emperor was considered undetermined and left out of the declaration. The wording was critical for the Japanese government to surrender unconditionally. In particular, the status of the emperor was the starting point for the Japanese officials, and they made it clear that without an assurance of the retention of the emperor, Japan could not accept the declaration. As a result, Japan initially rejected the declaration, but after the atomic bombing of Hiroshima and Nagasaki, and the Soviet's entrance into the war, Japan agreed to surrender unconditionally. Section 12 of the Potsdam Declaration states, "there has been established in accordance with the freely expressed will of the Japanese people a peacefully inclined and responsible government." The wording was purposely left ambiguous. The Japanese government interpreted the phrase as an allowance for a constitutional monarchy; thus, the emperor would be retained. It was a small window, but it made it easier for Japan to accept unconditional surrender despite the overwhelming events that spelt defeat for Japan.[14] Therefore, wording turned out to be important, and for the Japanese the interpretation of the words was even more critical.[15]

The discussion about the emperor and the imperial institution had just about covered all aspects of this complex problem, but the final treatment of the emperor was not resolved. Initially, the military did not agree with the State Department's lenient view towards the emperor. For the military, the successful completion of demilitarization meant not only the complete demobilization of Japan's armed forces, but also the arrest and trial of war criminals. Military and political

---

14. Richard B. Finn, *Winners in Peace: MacArthur, Yoshida, and Postwar Japan* (Berkeley: University of California Press, 1992), 30.

15. When asked by reporters to comment on the Potsdam Declaration, Prime Minister Kantaro Suzuki replied with one word, *mokusatsu*, which can be translated as "treating with silent contempt" or simply as "no comment." The word got out that the Japanese government response was the more negative "silent contempt." The US government was angered by this alleged response, and a few days later the atomic bomb was dropped on Hiroshima. Whether there is any correlation is problematic. For the full story, see William Craig, *The Fall of Japan: The Final Weeks of World War II in the Pacific* (New York: Dial Press, 1967).

leaders responsible for war crimes had to be held accountable. Emperor Hirohito, as the symbolic head of state, was deemed responsible. He consented to starting the war and other actions of the government and the military. The Japanese military often acted in the name of the emperor in banzai and kamikaze attacks. All sorts of coercive actions were undertaken, exploiting the mystique and authority of the emperor. Ultra-nationalistic elements in Japanese society acted under the banner of the emperor and engaged in violent acts. If the top military leaders are to be tried as war criminals, surely the emperor must be tried, so argued the planners in the departments of war and navy. Moreover, Hirohito was accused of making political decisions or inaction, which unnecessarily prolonged the war and caused countless civilians' casualties. All of these arguments contradicted the views of the State Department.[16]

On October 6, 1945, the views of those against the emperor were expressed in SWNCC-55/3, "Treatment of the Person of Hirohito, Emperor of Japan." It succinctly stated that Hirohito should be arrested, tried, and punished as a war criminal. The paper called for the assembly and transmittal of all available evidence so proceedings against Hirohito could begin.

An immediate pushback was SWNCC-55/6 (Revised), which said the emperor was not immune from being charged as a war criminal. But there should be no rush and all available evidence should be gathered by the Supreme Commander for the Allied Powers (SCAP), the headquarters of General Douglas MacArthur.[17] It argued the

---

16. The role of Emperor Hirohito in the Pacific War has been a point of controversy among historians, political scientists and journalists. See, for example, the following: Herbert P. Bix, *Hirohito and the Making of Modern Japan* (New York: Harper Collins Publisher, 2000); Stephen S. Large, *Emperor Hirohito and Showa Japan: A Political Biography* (New York: Routledge 1992); Edward S. Behr, *Hirohito: Behind the Myth* (New York: Villard Books, 1989); David Bergamini, *Japan's Imperial Conspiracy: How Emperor Hirohito Led Japan into War Against the West* (New York: William Morrow,1971).

17. Some writers prefer to use the acronym GHQ (General Headquarters) instead of SCAP. GHQ is the more generic term, including the headquarters that dealt with military operations and the headquarters that administered civil functions. SCAP, on the other hand, involves only civil matters. Although SCAP was composed of military personnel, it had a large number of civilians. Since this book is not focused on military operations, I have chosen to only use SCAP.

treatment of the emperor cannot be separated from the US objectives in Japan. Will it help to establish a democratic government in Japan, or will it deter? Ultimately, the Japanese government and the people should decide the emperor's fate.

The possibility of arresting the emperor was set aside by the final paper in this series, SWNCC-55/7 on June 12, 1946. The whole subject was removed from the agenda and further investigation was cancelled. Although the emperor, as a person, was no longer considered a war criminal, there was an absence of consensus on the role of the emperor and the role of the imperial institution—whether or not the emperor and the institution should be retained. Consequently, the status of the emperor was left open, but the planners still felt the need for constraints. They argued that if the emperor is retained, he should be permitted to act only on the advice of the cabinet, which would be responsible to the legislature. Ultimate control would always be in the hands of the representatives of the people. This principle of the throne being subordinate to the legislative branch was stated in papers produced by the early wartime subcommittees.

Before SWNCC-55/7 came out, which was the last of the SWNCC-55 series of papers, another report prepared by the Subcommittee for the Far East, SWNCC-209/1, was issued on March 6, 1946. In this report, prepared by several Japan specialists on the subcommittee, a detailed proposal is given on how the Japanese government should be encouraged to revise the Meiji Constitution by eliminating the divinity of the emperor and emperor worship and having greater transparency on the role of the monarchy. Since the majority of the Japanese wanted to retain the imperial system, the report concluded there was no rush in determining the ultimate role of the emperor, and it should be left to the Japanese people.

SWNCC-209/1 arrived at SCAP after it had already prepared its version of the draft constitution. SCAP was ready to present its draft constitution, which would result in a shocking incident (more on this incident in the next chapter). MacArthur and his staff knew about the content of SWNCC-209/1 since such a report goes through several drafts and was usually forwarded to the Joint Chiefs of Staff, and then to MacArthur's headquarters for further comments. Therefore,

MacArthur was aware of Washington's cautious handling of the emperor. SCAP had moved beyond revising the Meiji Constitution and well beyond the reforms envisaged by the planners in Washington.

The State-War-Navy Coordinating Committee did not move forward on the status of the emperor for more than six months. There are several reasons for this. Working with three departments was more complicated than anticipated, and the sharing of information took time. For all departments, the treatment of the emperor was a low priority. The demobilization of the Japanese armed forces and the pressing economic conditions were more critical. In addition, military advisors were dissatisfied with the State Department's views on the handling of the emperor. And the army was in no hurry because they would soon be in charge of the Occupation, allowing them to have a say on how the emperor was treated.

The majority of the SWNCC documents appeared after the war had ended. Their intended purpose was to serve as guidelines for the Occupation. The SWNCC-209 series, for example, referred back to the earlier proposals of State Department planners on how the emperor should be used to accomplish the objectives of the Occupation. Of all the SWNCC documents, the most important was "The Reform of the Japanese Governmental System" (SWNCC-228) of January 7, 1946, which became the basis for the draft of the Japanese Constitution. It allowed the Japanese government to initiate constitutional reforms and independently take the initiative.[18] Although the Japanese government was given the opportunity to revise and amend the constitution, it was under controlled conditions. However, this option was soon eliminated when the American planners took over the writing of the draft constitution.

In essence, the US government left the status of the emperor to the discretion of SCAP. MacArthur was cognizant of the SWNCC documents, but he had his own ideas of how to handle the emperor. He did not want to treat the emperor as a war criminal or abolish the imperial institution. The emperor was to be used, not eliminated.

---

18. *https://www.ndl.go.jp* > shiryo.

MacArthur wrote the following about the emperor to Dr. Kenzo Takayanagi, Chairman of the Commission on the Constitution:

> The preservation of the emperor system was my fixed idea. It was inherent and integral to Japanese political and cultural survival. The vicious efforts to destroy the person of the emperor and thereby abolish the system became one of the most dangerous menaces that threatened the successful rehabilitation of the nation.[19]

How did the "fixed idea" of preserving the emperor system come about? From the early stages of the Occupation, MacArthur had already decided to retain the emperor and not have him tried as a war criminal. He determined the status of the emperor much earlier than Article 9. A major influence on MacArthur's thinking was the studies done by Brigadier General Bonner F. Fellers. Fellers served as MacArthur's military secretary and was chief of his psychological warfare operations. He served under MacArthur in the Philippines before and during the war. A large number of military officers, including Fellers, accompanied MacArthur to Tokyo. They were called the "Bataan Boys." But even among these officers, MacArthur confided with only a few, and Fellers was one of those he sought for advice on matters pertaining to the emperorship.

When the writings of Fellers are compared with the pronouncements of MacArthur, the origins of the arguments and conclusions used by the general are clearly discernible. Fellers argued that the enemy should not be provoked by attacking the emperor. This was consistent with the US war policy of not attacking the imperial palace in Tokyo. Everywhere, Tokyo was bombed and firebombed, but the imperial palace remained unscathed. The Japanese regarded their emperor with religious awe and

---

19. Kenzo Takayanagi, "Some Reminiscences of Japan's Commission on the Constitution," in *The Constitution of Japan: Its First Twenty Years, 1947-67,* ed. Dan Fenno Henderson (Seattle: University of Washington Press, 1968), 79.

would fight to the death if the emperor was attacked. Fellers made the following argument:

> ...However, to dethrone, or hang, the emperor would cause a tremendous and violent reaction from all Japanese. Hanging of the Emperor to them would be comparable to the crucifixion of Christ to us. All would fight to die like ants. The position of the gangster militarists would be strengthened immeasurably. The war would be unduly prolonged; our losses heavier than otherwise would be necessary.[20]

Fellers said a "wedge" must be driven between the emperor and the people on the one hand, and the Tokyo gangster militarists on the other. He summarized his thoughts:

> An independent Japanese army responsible only to the Emperor is a permanent menace to peace. But the mystic holds the Emperor has on his people and the spiritual strength of the Shinto faith properly directed need not be dangerous. The Emperor can be made a force for good and peace provided Japan is totally defeated and the military clique destroyed.[21]

It was the end of January 1946, and the Japanese government was slow and still had not produced a revision of the Meiji Constitution. MacArthur was anxious to have a constitution that met the objectives of the Occupation. He firmly believed the emperor was needed for the Occupation to be successful. The imperial institution would help to galvanize the Japanese government and the people, supporting and implementing the occupation's policies. Therefore, provisions for the retention of the emperor must be in the constitution. There were two sets of pressures on the government, one internal and the other external.

---

20. John W. Dower, *Embracing Defeat: Japan in the Wake of World War II* (New York: W. W. Norton, 1999), 282-83.

21. Dower, *Embracing*, 283.

Domestically, polls indicated the Japanese people wanted revision and to have their own government's commission do the drafting. Meanwhile, Japanese leaders urged immediate but limited revisions along the lines of the Meiji Constitution; it would lean toward the conservative right, something SCAP wanted to avoid. The external threat came from the Far Eastern Commission (FEC). The FEC was composed of thirteen allied countries and operated out of Washington, DC. It was beginning to assert its views and was eager to take control of the Occupation of Japan. The top leadership circle of the FEC was the Allied Council for Japan, which was situated in Tokyo. The council consisted of the United States, the United Kingdom, China, and the Soviet Union with each having veto power. Already, some of the countries in the FEC had voiced their opinion about the emperor and the imperial institution— they would prefer to have both abolished. As it turned out, neither the FEC nor the Allied Council for Japan were active until early 1946, and even after they met, their influence was minimal. Nevertheless, the domestic and external pressures were there, so MacArthur had to make his move.

After considerable pressure, the "Matsumoto Draft" was produced, but SCAP rejected it as totally unacceptable. At that moment, MacArthur decided to draft a completely new model constitution. He had specific instructions in mind on what should be in the new constitution. They were hurriedly written in pencil on a yellow legal pad. General Courtney Whitney was ordered to carry out the following provisions, often referred to as the "three principles:"

I. The Emperor is at the head of the State. His succession is dynastic. His duties and powers will be exercised in accordance with the Constitution and responsive to the basic will of the people as provided therein.

II. War as a sovereign right of the nation is abolished. Japan renounces it as an instrumentality for settling its disputes and even for preserving its own security. It relies upon the higher ideals, which are now stirring the world for its defense and its protection. No Japanese Army, Navy, or Air Force will ever be authorized, and no rights of belligerency will ever be conferred upon any Japanese force.

III. The feudal system will cease. No rights of peerage except those of the Imperial family will extend beyond the lives of those now existent. No patent of nobility will from this time forth embody within itself any National or Civic power of government. Pattern budget after British system.[22]

MacArthur's three principles are a completely new set of constitutional provisions. They are not revisions or amendments but are new constitutional articles. Comparing the first principle cited above with the first four articles of the Meiji Constitution previously cited shows the extent of the change. What is obvious when one looks at these articles is their connection with what the planners of the State Department had worked on and how they are linked with some of the SWNCC documents. To see how the proposals pertaining to the emperor became part of the new constitution, the following two articles of the Constitution of Japan are provided for comparison:

Article 1. The Emperor shall be the symbol of the State and of the unity of the People, deriving his position from the will of the people with whom resides sovereign power.

Article 2. The Imperial Throne shall be dynastic and succeeded in accordance with the Imperial House Law passed by the Diet.

Now, comparing the two articles about the emperor in the present Japanese Constitution with the first of MacArthur's three principles in the SCAP draft constitution, the words and phraseology are almost identical or very similar. The planning of the State Department was significant. What we have today in the new constitution on the role and functions of the emperor is what many of the early planners had envisioned.

---

22. Supreme Commander for the Allied Powers, Government Section. *Political Reorientation of Japan, September 1945 to September 1948* (Washington, DC: Government Printing Office, 1949), 1:102. *https://www.ndl.go.jp* > shiryo.

There was a progression in how the potential issues were handled. In the early pre-surrender documents, the pronouncements were generalities, but in later meetings, the documents became increasingly specific and practical. The discussions moved from general concerns to proposed solutions to specific anticipated postwar problems. And as we have seen, it moved from civilian planners to increasingly military planners.

In the following chapter, to better understand how an article such as Article 9 developed, the process by which the Constitution of Japan was drafted will be examined in detail. Previously, the status of the emperor was analyzed with a focus on pre-surrender planning, but with Article 9, the emphasis will be on post-surrender planning.

AUTHORSHIP AND ARTICLE 9

CHAPTER TWO

How the Japanese Constitution came about is a fascinating story. Its origin is a major point of contention. Critics view it as an alien document because it was written by American personnel of the Government Section of SCAP. Sometimes, it is derisively called the "MacArthur Constitution." The American handprint is evident in the preamble, which is one long sentence, for it closely resembles the preamble of the US Constitution. It reads as follows:

> We, the Japanese people, acting through our duly elected representatives in the National Diet, determined that we shall secure for ourselves and our posterity the fruits of peaceful cooperation with all nations and the blessings of liberty throughout this land, and resolved that never again shall we be visited with the horrors of war through the action of government, do proclaim that sovereign power resides with the people and do firmly establish this Constitution.

Initially, the Americans only wanted to revise the former constitution, the Meiji Constitution of 1889. Of course, the changes had to be extensive; cosmetic changes would not suffice. This is what the prewar planners of the State Department had recommended. To revise and not replace, was in accord with the overall decision of the US administration, using the indirect approach in governing Japan. In contrast, the direct approach was used in occupied Germany. Germany was divided into four occupation zones (United States, United Kingdom, France, and Soviet Union) with the Allied powers already having their troops stationed on German soil. Each Allied power had its own military government, which set and implemented its own policies. In the indirect method, which Borton insisted on, the Japanese government took the initiative. Following American directives, they made the instructions their own, and used their bureaucracy to implement the project or program. The United States would control Japan through the Japanese government.

SCAP knew that it had to work closely with the Japanese government if it wanted to successfully achieve constitutional reform, its most important task in the democratization of Japan. What took place next was a tragedy and a fiasco. First, let us look at the tragedy. On October 4, 1945, General MacArthur took the first step in revising the Meiji Constitution.He asked Prince Fumimaro Konoe, who was the minister of state without portfolio and the deputy prime minister in the Prince Naruhiko Higashikuni cabinet, to lead a committee on constitutional revision. Konoe, an aristocratic politician, was prime minister twice in the late 1930s and during the war. The use of old-line politicians to lead the way in making revisions had serious consequences, but SCAP had few options because many of the experienced political leaders were tainted with wartime involvement. That was the case with Konoe, as he headed the government at the time of military expansionism. Before long, his past caught up with him and led to his demise and eventual tragedy.

The purpose of Konoe's committee was to amend the Meiji Constitution into a more democratic document. Konoe discussed the revisions of the Meiji Constitution with George Atcheson, Jr., the highest State Department official in Tokyo and advisor to MacArthur. Atcheson suggested that SCAP follow his recommendations and informally guide the Japanese efforts to reform their constitution. Although SCAP acknowledged Atcheson's recommendations, it decided to reject his advice after concluding that the revision of the Meiji Constitution was not enough. Atcheson regularly communicated with the State Department, and MacArthur considered this a hindrance since he wanted to avoid any State Department interference. He believed the implementation of a constitutional revision to be the prerogative of SCAP. Given the direction that the Japanese were already taking, it seemed inevitable that the Japanese would produce an unacceptable document.

Meanwhile, the Higashikuni cabinet got into a dispute over the occupation policy of repealing the 1925 Peace Preservation Law. It was a repressive law, an effort at thought control, and meant especially to suppress socialists and communists. For the old-line politicians, this was asking too much. The cabinet felt it could not carry out MacArthur's order and promptly resigned after eight weeks in office. Even with this disruption, Prince Konoe continued to work with his committee and incessantly pursued his efforts to revise the constitution with Kijuro Shidehara, the new prime minister. He began to face criticism for his role during the war and for being a suspected war criminal. Within his own committee, Konoe faced opposition as members resented his total acceptance of the liberal views of SCAP. With all these criticisms swirling around Konoe, SCAP decided on November 1st to withdraw its support of the prince.

The official purge list came out with Konoe as a Class A war criminal. His work on the draft came to a standstill. Two weeks later, the proud prince, facing possible imprisonment as a war criminal and having been rejected by SCAP, committed suicide by taking poison.[23]

At about the same time, the Japanese government had another committee working on revising the constitution. It ended in a fiasco. The Constitutional Problem Investigation Committee was formed on October 27, 1945, and was chaired by Dr. Joji Matsumoto. Matsumoto was a legal scholar and politician. The committee, often referred to as the Matsumoto Committee, was composed of several academics from Kyoto. They met for seven general meetings and had fifteen work sessions and were known for working in secrecy. In contrast to Prince Konoe, Matsumoto was stubborn, some would say arrogant, refusing to listen to SCAP and deciding to work independently. He took a narrow view of only making a few changes to the Meiji Constitution and believed radical reform was unnecessary. MacArthur was perturbed because the committee was slow in its work. There was concern about timeliness. The Far Eastern Commission (FEC) was being formed and soon the United States would be joined by other FEC members,

---

23. Dale M. Hellegers, *We, the Japanese People: World War II and the Origins of the Japanese Constitution. Vol. 2 Tokyo* (Stanford: Stanford University Press, 2001). A massive study, volume 2 covers the planning and decision-making that took place in Tokyo.

especially the major powers—the United Kingdom, China, and the Soviet Union. The US would lose sole control of the Occupation of Japan, as the other FEC members would have their say. General Whitney, chief of the Government Section, urged MacArthur to act before the FEC started to meet. [24]

Dr. Joji Matsumoto

One reason why the Matsumoto Committee was slow was that it was working on two draft proposals. Proposal A was "Gist of the Revision of the Constitution," which eventually became known as the Matsumoto Draft. Proposal B was "Tentative Revision of the Constitution." Somehow, the Japanese newspaper *Mainichi Shimbun* got hold of Proposal B, which proposed a few changes, essentially maintaining the status quo. Proposal A would not have been any better, for it was just as conservative, in fact, more so. The *Mainichi* printed the draft the next day, on February 1, 1946, and it resulted in a public uproar with severe criticisms from the national media. Many felt that it did not meet

24. Theodore H. McNelly, "'Induced Revolution': The Policy and Process of Constitutional Reform in Occupied Japan," in Ward and Sakamoto, *Democratizing Japan, 79.*

the needs of the people. Through the negative feedback, MacArthur learned about the inadequacies of the "Matsumoto Draft" and that the Matsumoto Committee was headed in the wrong direction.

From the inception of the Konoe and Matsumoto committees to the final approval of the draft by the Diet (roughly from the fall of 1945 to March 1946), there was a surprising outpour of at least a dozen constitutional proposals from private and public organizations. The Japan Communist Party (*Kyosanto*), the Japan Liberal Party (*Jiyuto*), the Japan Progressive Party (*Shinpoto*), and the Japan Socialist Party (*Shakaito*) announced their proposals for revision. Professional associations such as the All Japan Lawyers' Association submitted their draft of constitutional revision. Private organizations, including the Constitutional Research Association (*Kempo Kenkyukai*) and the Constitutional Discussion Group (*Kempo Kondankai*), contributed their ideas. Individuals also published their draft constitution or sent in their proposals. Several proposals with liberal and progressive ideas got the attention of SCAP. Of particular interest was the Constitutional Research Association draft with its "outstanding liberal provisions." Looking back at these draft proposals, it is remarkable and surprising how close some of them came to what we have today in the Japanese Constitution. Unfortunately, the Matsumoto Committee was not interested in any of these proposals; it did not want to look at other alternatives and was completely out of touch with Japanese society. [25]

It took the Matsumoto Committee three months before it submitted its draft constitution on February 8, 1946. The long wait frustrated MacArthur, and he was further annoyed when the *Mainichi* "scoop" revealed only minor changes had been made to the Meiji Constitution. This delay gave MacArthur time to think about Japan's postwar constitution, and he came to the conclusion the revision was not enough. It had to be a new constitution. He and his staff determined that the Japanese government was incapable of drafting a constitution. He would have to initiate a model constitution that included the principles he desired. Therefore, even before the Matsumoto Draft was submitted, he instructed General Whitney on February 3 to start on a new draft constitution and to include his three principles. It was a bold

---

25. Dower, *Embracing*, 348, 356-67.

decision and showed the complete authority wielded by MacArthur. Washington never gave MacArthur instructions or authorization to draft a constitution, and MacArthur did not inform the State and War departments about his plan to draft a new constitution. It took Washington by surprise.

Listed below are the previously mentioned Principles I and III of MacArthur's three principles. They are presented in outlined form for purposes of discussion. Principle II will be discussed in the section on Article 9.

Principle I

The Emperor is at the head of the State. His succession is dynastic. His duties and powers will be exercised in accordance with the Constitution and responsive to the basic will of the people as provided therein.

Principle III

The feudal system of Japan will cease. No rights of peerage except those of the Imperial family will extend beyond the lives of those now existent. No patent of nobility will from this time forth embody within itself any National or Civic power of government. Pattern budget after British system.

General MacArthur had a timeline. The draft constitution had to be completed by February 12 because of the pending FEC meeting with the possibility of strong outside interference. On February 4, 1946, the Government Section was ordered to draft a new constitution in eight days. Amazingly, the Government Section accomplished this task in six days. General Whitney called the week-long session a "constitutional convention."

The stirring story has been told many times—a small steering committee with seven subcommittees was able to write a constitution in under a week. The entire team was composed of twenty-four, mostly junior officers and eight civilians. It was led by Colonel Charles L. Kades, Deputy Chief of the Government Section. He was part of the steering committee along with Commander Alfred R. Hussey, Jr. and Lieutenant Colonel Milo E. Rowell. The Government Section was small and differed from other sections in SCAP in terms of personnel. The SCAP bureaucracy was typically staffed with career officers who had fought with MacArthur in the Pacific War. Whereas the Government Section was staffed with officers in uniforms who were professionals with specialized skills and experience in civilian life.Although they were highly educated, most of the members of the subcommittees knew little about Japan. Kades admitted he knew almost nothing about Japan, and whatever he knew was from reading the newspaper. There were no constitutional law specialists, but there were four lawyers (Kades, Hussey, Rowell, and Lieutenant Colonel Frank E. Hays). Kades was a New Deal administrator and worked in the Treasury Department of the Roosevelt administration. Hussey, Rowell, and Kades were Harvard graduates and undoubtedly were products of the high-minded liberalism of the 1930s. The Government Section was accused of harboring many New Deal idealists. The rest of the officers on the committee are listed by their profession or civilian job:

- academics - Lieutenant Colonel Pieter Roest, Lieutenant Colonel Cecil Tilton, and Dr. Cyrus H. Peake

- journalists - Navy Lieutenant Osborne Hauge and Harry Emerson Wildes

- former congressman and governor of Puerto Rico - Commander Guy J. Swope

- foreign service officer - Navy Lieutenant Richard Poole

- public administration specialist - First Lieutenant Milton J. Esman

- Wall Street investor - Major Frank Rizzo

- civilian intelligence specialist - Lieutenant Commander Roy L. Malcolm[26]

Colonel Charles L. Kades
Courtesy of Gordon Prange Collection

The Government Section worked all day and night. To help with the language problem, Nisei (second-generation Japanese Americans) from the Military Intelligence Service were attached to SCAP. The Nisei were recently commissioned second lieutenants, made possible by the War Department's decision to end its discriminatory policy. Previously, Nisei graduates of the army's language school were awarded sergeant's stripes, whereas Caucasian students with fewer skills were commissioned as lieutenants. Now, Nisei graduates of the language school were commissioned officers. These officers did not participate in policy planning but served as translators and interpreters.

---

26. Dower, 364-65.

There were four women in the group, and one—Beate Sirota, a twenty-two-year-old low-level official—had an unusual background. Sirota was brought up in Japan and was fluent in Japanese. Her family had migrated to Japan to escape Nazi oppression. Sirota's father, a Ukrainian Jew, was a noted pianist and had taken a position as a professor at a music academy. Her parents wanted Beate to attend college in America, so she enrolled at Mills College in Oakland, California. Then, the war began, and Sirota was separated from her parents for the duration of the war. During this period, she worked for the US government translating Japanese broadcasts. But Sirota wanted to go to Japan to be with her parents, so she got a job as an interpreter for SCAP and returned home.

Beate Sirota

Sirota was appointed to the subcommittee for civil rights, and since she was the only woman in the subcommittee, she was assigned to work on women and other human rights. Sirota knew the traditional and subservient roles of Japanese women, and what they desperately needed. She began the assignment by getting hold of a jeep and driving to the Diet Library and any other libraries she could find with reference books on constitutional law. Sirota studied these books, and when asked by higher-rank officers to defend the inclusion of clauses guaranteeing gender equality, she was ready. Through her persistence, she persuaded the once disinterested, middle-aged officers to include women's rights in the draft. The equality of the sexes clause Sirota helped to insert into the draft is a guarantee not found in the US Constitution. With her bilingual skills, Sirota was able to make the necessary translation with all its nuances from English to Japanese. She did her assignment exceedingly well, as attested to by Articles 14 and 24 in Chapter III of the Japanese Constitution. Her contribution remains intact. Overall, the interaction on human rights loosened up the proceedings and allowed the discussion and eventual inclusion of other innovative reforms.[27]

The team members depended on a variety of sources to compose the draft constitution. For the members working on the people's rights and responsibilities (Chapter III), similar to Sirota, they consulted any constitutional references they could find on individual rights and responsibilities. This section of the draft ended with some thirty articles, the most extensive in the draft constitution. Siroita, with the help of Lieutenant Milton Esman, obtained copies of the constitutions for about twelve countries. Japanese sources were consulted with the help of translators. The drafts submitted by the Liberal, Progressive, and Socialist Parties were useful, as they contained progressive provisions that were in agreement with the thinking of the drafters. Another Japanese source used was the model constitution proposed by the Constitution Research Society.

Of the sources generated in Tokyo and those emanating from Washington, the key documents were MacArthur's three principles and the SWNCC directives. In his directive, MacArthur insisted on making the emperor accountable to the Japanese people and abolishing the inherited power of Japan's aristocracy. This became the wording for

---

27. Beate Sirota Gordon, *The Only Women in the Room: A Memoir of Japan, Human Rights, and the Arts* (Chicago: University of Chicago Press, 1997). In 1948, Sirota married Lieutenant Joseph Gordon, who was also with SCAP. After she left government service, she became a performing arts presenter and women's rights activist. Sirota Gordon became an iconic figure in Japanese feminist movement and was given a heroine's welcome whenever she visited Japan.

Chapter I. MacArthur also wanted to eliminate Japan's ability to wage war, and Chapter II, on the renunciation of war, was the result. His insistence on the British parliamentary system and a unitary legislative body were carried out, but the unitary system was later dropped in favor of bicameralism. It was one of the few compromises SCAP was willing to accept. He also asked for a budget system patterned after the British. It should be remembered the Japanese themselves were familiar with many democratic institutions and practices. The Meiji legislative body and the cabinet were based on the British model, and other European borrowings. In the 1920s, Japan underwent the so-called "Taisho Democracy," where political parties competed in free elections and opposition movements emerged. This was the heyday of the democratic movement in Japan, but it ended with the rise of right-wing nationalism and militarism in the 1930s. Nevertheless, the Japanese became familiar with the democratic system of government.

In the background, was SWNCC-228 ("Reform of the Japanese Governmental System") and the many papers generated by the prewar planners. The influence of SWNCC-228 was especially profound. It was used by the drafters as a reference document, setting forth the constitutional reforms that should be carried out by the Japanese government. Kades said that each subcommittee was charged "with the responsibility of conforming its draft to the general principles set forth in SWNCC-228."[28] Many of the advocated reforms, such as civilian authority over the military, became provisions in the Japanese Constitution.

At the conclusion of the "constitutional convention," SCAP had a brand-new draft constitution. General Whitney, as head of the Government Section, was ready to meet with the Japanese officials, who two days earlier submitted their version of the revised Meiji Constitution. On February 13, 1946, Gen. Whitney met with Shigeru Yoshida (at that time foreign minister), Minister of State Joji Matsumoto, Jiro Shirasu, councillor of the Central Liaison Office, and an officially designated interpreter. He informed them that SCAP totally rejects the "Gist of the Revision of the Constitution" (Matsumoto Draft).

---

28. Charles L. Kades, "The American Role in Revising Japan's Imperial Constitution." *Political Science Quarterly* 104, no. 2 (Summer 1989): 226.

Whitney then handed over four copies of the SCAP/MacArthur draft of the constitution to the shocked Japanese. All this time, the Japanese officials were working on amending the Meiji Constitution, so it was a surprise to see the SCAP draft. They assumed that if the Americans had any suggestions, it would be in the form of revisions. They were not expecting a new constitution. Whitney made it clear the Japanese leaders had little choice but to accept the SCAP draft. It was the only way to ensure the retention of the emperor. Furthermore, Whitney said MacArthur would circumvent the Japanese government and take the constitution directly to the Japanese people if the government did not endorse the SCAP draft constitution. Some writers believe Whitney hinted that bodily harm would come to the emperor, but there is no evidence of such a coercive threat. Matsumoto claimed Whitney made the threat, but he misinterpreted Whitney's statement. Undeniably, the pressure was on the Japanese government to accept the SCAP draft, and they did accept it. The Matsumoto Draft turned out to be a flop, thus ending the fiasco.

Matsumoto still insisted his draft of the constitution could be accepted with a few additional changes, but SCAP felt it was deficient in too many ways. The two most important provisions to MacArthur were not included—the emperor is only a "symbol" of the state and a war-renouncing clause. These omissions and the attempt by the Shidehara government to downgrade the war-renouncing clause were objectionable to SCAP.

A little over two weeks after General Whitney had made his presentation of the SCAP draft, the cabinet presented the Japanese draft with no English translation on the morning of March 4, 1946. The passage of time gave the impression that the cabinet had made the draft their own. The Japanese officials had the tendency from the very beginning to give the appearance that the draft was their creation. In this case, it was merely a Japanese version of the SCAP draft. Even so, the Americans found the Japanese officials had changed several words, altering their meaning. Hence, the Japanese version had to be reworked. Colonel Kades and Tatsuo Sato, from the cabinet's Bureau of Legislation, worked on the wording of the text and produced a new draft, which returned essentially to the original SCAP document. The effort took thirty hours of work, translating the text from Japanese to

English and back to Japanese. Sato brought along two interpreters, while Kades had the support of about sixteen American officers with assistance provided by Nisei translators and interpreters. In any translation, there will be situations where there is a choice in the word to be used. For example, the words "people" and "sovereignty," in each case, can be translated by two similar words in Japanese that have different connotations. The Japanese chose the word that fitted in with their traditional way of thinking and their culture, and as it turned out, the meaning of the word differed from what the Americans wanted.[29]

Two days later, on March 6, 1946, three consequential pronouncements were made. First, Shidehara announced the SCAP draft, now called the "Draft for a Revised Constitution," was the "handiwork" of the cabinet. It allowed the Japanese officials to accept and claim SCAP products as their own. The cabinet endorsed the "handiwork" or draft constitution, and it was submitted to the Diet. Second, at the same time, Emperor Hirohito announced in an imperial rescript the acceptance of the draft constitution. He understood how the draft would ensure the protection of his position and the imperial institution. Finally, on the same day, General MacArthur announced his approval of the emperor's decision and that of the government to accept the draft.[30] For the first time, the draft constitution was revealed to the public. In all these pronouncements, no mention was made of SCAP involvement. The media was told not to talk about it. It would make it easier in the forthcoming Diet debates if this document was seen as a Japanese product. But without a doubt, this was clearly a SCAP draft.

From the time of the release of the SCAP draft constitution in February to its promulgation in November 1946, eight months would pass. The proposed constitution was not quietly approved. Instead, it went through a series of proceedings, where it was debated and amended.

---

29. Dower, *Embracing*, 379-82. There is controversy over the translation of certain words and its implication for interpreting the Japanese Constitution. See: Kyoko Inoue, *MacArthur's Japanese Constitution: A Linguistic and Cultural Study of its Making* (Chicago: University of Chicago Press, 1991.

30. Dower, 384-87.

A general election was held on April 10, 1946, the first election after World War II. The election weakened the Shidehara government and delayed work on the draft in the lower house of the Diet. Meanwhile, the "Draft for a Revised Constitution" was brought before the Privy Council. The Privy Council was an advisory council to the emperor. It was abolished the following year when the new Constitution of Japan became effective. There was also a delay in the Privy Council due to changes in the government. In the aftermath of the election, the two conservative parties that formed the coalition government decided to pull away from Shidehara. This splinter, plus disagreement with SCAP over occupation policies, caused the Shidehara cabinet to resign en bloc on April 22. With the political turmoil, it took six weeks before the new Yoshida cabinet was installed. After all these delays, the "Draft for a Revised Constitution" was finally approved overwhelmingly in early June after the Privy Council had met eight times. The Privy Council sessions were sparked with emotional discussions on the "national polity," the emperor, and the renunciation of war provisions in Article 9. Despite the doubts and apprehension expressed, many members still believed the throne with all its splendor would continue to be retained—this was enough, and they found the draft acceptable.[31]

---

31. Dower, 388-90.

Kijuro Shidehara

Courtesy of the National Diet Library

With the opening of a new session of the Diet, the Yoshida cabinet submitted the now-renamed "Bill for Revision of the Imperial Constitution" for review on June 20, 1946. It is important to note that this final draft was written in colloquial Japanese rather than the formal style that is difficult to read and only the educated elites could understand. The common people could read it now. Henceforth, all official documents and laws would be in ordinary Japanese.[32]

The revision bill was referred to the Committee on the Bill for Revision of the Imperial Constitution of the House of Representatives, which was chaired by Hitoshi Ashida. Ashida was a former diplomat who went into politics and was prime minister for a short period in 1948. Two of the proposals submitted by this committee became part of the present Constitution—Article 25, a commitment to ensuring an adequate standard of living for the Japanese people and Article 26, an

---

32. Dower, 387.

extension of free compulsory education. But more important was the approval to include a crucial clause, the so-called "Ashida amendment," at the beginning of the second paragraph of Article 9. The clause began, "In order to accomplish the aim of the preceding paragraph." How this clause affected the interpretation of the article will be explained in the following section on Article 9.

Hitoshi Ashida

The House of Representatives overwhelmingly passed the revision bill. The next step was the upper house, the House of Peers, where the bill was deliberated for about a month, resulting in four minor revisions. At the end of the deliberation, the House of Peers overwhelmingly approved the "Bill for Revision of the Imperial Constitution" as revised and sent it back to the House of Representatives, where it was again decisively approved. Up to this point, the Diet deliberation had taken over three months. Observers have debated the importance of these discussions. It is agreed the revisions and additions were minor, but the debates were wide-ranging, and there was a good airing of opinions. The revised bill was then sent to the Privy Council, which gave its approval. Finally, the "Bill for Revision of the Imperial Constitution," after receiving the Emperor's approval, was promulgated as the Constitution of Japan on November 3, 1946.

With the adoption of the new constitution, a massive public education campaign was launched by the Japanese government. Through the support of SCAP, it informed the Japanese people about the provisions of the new constitution. The Constitution Popularization Society was formed in December l, 1946 and was headed by Ashida. It was tasked with training government employees to carry out the educational objective and producing literature to promote the constitution. The government issued twenty million copies of "New Constitution, Bright Life," a booklet extolling the virtues of democracy with a highly optimistic and idealistic view of the new Japan. The huge number was to ensure that every household in Japan received a copy.[33] Of course, this was political propaganda. But SCAP insisted on it, and it became successful. The overwhelming support of the populace for the Constitution endured for several decades, and there were no serious attempts to revise the Constitution until the mid-1950s.

Once the Occupation ended, serious debates began about the nature of the Occupation and specifically about the process by which the Constitution was formulated and instituted. The critics focused on foreign authorship and how the Constitution was "imposed" on the Japanese. The key word is "imposed," meaning it was forced on the hapless Japanese, who had little or no input—it was a fait accompli. This notion of an "imposed constitution" is the focal point of the conservatives' argument. They argue the text of the constitution does not take into consideration Japan's culture and tradition and deprives the emperor of his legal authority, thus undermining national unity and identity. The LDP and all of its prime ministers, starting with Nobusuke Kishi (1957-1960) and continuing to his grandson, Shinzo Abe (2006-2007, 2012-2020) and beyond, have followed the "imposed" argument.

Besides the style and wording of the Constitution, the procedure by which it was established has come under criticism. It is said the constitution was a neocolonial project of the Americans and was forced on the powerless Japanese by military might. The argument is cogently put forth by *Nippon Kaigi* (Japan Conference), a highly nationalistic, right-wing organization. According to their point of view,

33. *https://www.ndl.go.jp* > shiryo.

the constitution was instituted when Japan did not have its sovereignty. The Japanese Constitution is not an expression of the free will of the Japanese people. It should have been done by self-determination with no foreign interference.

In contrast to the "imposed constitution" argument, there are those who emphasize the active role played by the Japanese in constitution drafting; they did it freely because they wanted democratic reforms. Constitutional scholars such as Shoichi Koseki and Kenzo Takayanagi have shown how the Japanese contributed positively to their collaborative efforts with the Americans. When given the opportunity, individuals and organizations presented their version of the desired constitution, and surprisingly, some of their ideas are what we have today in the Japanese Constitution. What direct impact the public proposals had is problematic, but at least they were expressed. In consultations and negotiations with SCAP officials and parliamentary deliberations, Japanese officials did have some input. Granted, the changes and additions made were minor, even cosmetic. Still, even small changes could have consequences. It could lead to new interpretations.

In the discussions between Japanese and SCAP officials, the text of the proposed constitution was edited and retranslated. As previously mentioned, certain words changed when translated and replaced by other words that seemed similar but had different meanings. We all know words can have several meanings, and what meaning you choose depends on your cultural background. Furthermore, words or phrases could be inserted or removed and that could change the interpretation of the clause. The Bible, for example, has several translations. With each translation, certain words and passages have changed. This has led to new insights that are interpreted differently by theologians, pastors, and lay leaders. Hence, changes could occur in a translation or interpretation.

Even though the Diet members had the opportunity and made some contributions, historian John Dower cautioned that the parliamentary deliberations were closely supervised by SCAP and were an example of

"Japanizing democracy."[34] "Guided democracy" is the more popular term. The Japanese were encouraged to use democratic procedures, but the whole process was carefully guided. The presence of American officials was keenly felt. Approximately, thirty changes and additions were made to the SCAP draft. It is believed they were allowed because they were in accord with what MacArthur and his staff wanted. The Japanese political leaders were free to express their views as long as they fit in with the objectives of the Occupation.

To summarize, the authorship of many articles in the present Japanese Constitution can be traced back to the committees of the State Department and to SWNCC, the inter-agency committee. Two key written instructions provided the basis for the draft constitution, and with minor changes and additions became the Constitution of Japan. The two principal instructions used by the Government Section were SWNCC-228 and MacArthur's three principles.

SWNCC-228, as we have seen, is a remarkable document. Prepared by Japan specialists in the Subcommittee for the Far East of SWNCC and completed on November 27, 1945, it became the basic guideline for the Occupation of Japan. The Joint Chiefs of Staff transmitted it to MacArthur on January 11, 1946. There is no known reason why it took so long to officially send it, but MacArthur knew of its content. SWNCC-228 was more informational than a direct order. To what extent MacArthur relied on SWNCC-228 is problematic. He had preconceived ideas he wanted to see in the Constitution but was still open to suggestions. When his preferences coincided with those stated in SWNCC-228, it reinforced his position. Comparing the language and principles in SWNCC-228 with MacArthur's three principles reveals a close affinity between the two. It can be said that SWNCC-228 played a part in the development of MacArthur's "three principles" and was an important source for the Government Section's drafters. Therefore, SWNCC-228 is a progenitor of the present Japanese Constitution.

What other antecedents were there for the MacArthur draft? Previously, the possible impact of SWNCC-209/1 has been noted.

---

34. Dower, *Embracing*, 391. For further criticisms, see Glenn D. Hook and Gavan McCormack, *Japan's Contested Constitution: Documents and Analysis* (New York: Routledge, 2001).

There were other sources of instructions, specifically the US Initial Post-Surrender Policy for Japan (SWNCC-150/4) of August 31, 1945, and the Basic Directive for Post-Surrender Military Government in Japan Proper (SWNCC-52/7) of November 3, 1945. Both documents directed MacArthur to use the emperor and not to eliminate the monarchy. The basic directive stated as follows, "It is contemplated, however, that unless you deem it necessary, or are instructed to the contrary you will not establish direct military government, but will exercise your powers so far as compatible with the accomplishment of your mission through the Emperor of Japan or the Japanese Government."[35] Nevertheless, these communications from Washington omitted certain issues, and the directions were often vaguely stated and open to interpretation. MacArthur considered these to be guidance rather than directives. It gave him considerable freedom in the formulation and implementation of policy measures. He boldly set forth his agenda.

Timing played a critical part in the process of drafting and approving the Japanese Constitution. The deliberate drawn-out process of planning, the rush to have it drafted, the period of pause, the protracted approval process, and the heated Diet deliberation all had a part in putting together the constitution. A brief timeline is presented below to summarize the process. These are events that had direct or indirect effects on the efforts to amend or revise the status of the emperor and Article 9.

TIMELINE[36]

1945

Oct. 4   MacArthur initiates the move to revise the Meiji Constitution. Konoe is chosen to head the constitutional revision committee.

Oct. 8   Konoe consults with Atcheson.

Oct. 25   Matsumoto Committee established.

---

35. Kokuritsu kokkai toshokan (National Diet LIbrary), part 1, sec. 2. *https://www.ndl.go.jp* > shiryo.

36. Excluded from the timeline are meetings of committees, agencies, and officials that dealt primarily with other substantive issues, such as human rights, or were general discussions.

1946

Jan. 24   Shidehara consults with MacArthur on emperor and Article 9.

Feb. 1   *Mainichi Shimbun* "scoop."

Feb. 3   MacArthur's three principles; Gov. Section ordered to draft constitution.

Feb. 4   Gov. Section begins work on draft.

Feb. 8   Japanese government submits Matsumoto Draft to SCAP.

Feb. 10   Gov. Section completes draft.

Feb. 13   SCAP rejects Matsumoto Draft; SCAP draft introduced.

Feb. 22   cabinet accepts SCAP draft.

Feb. 26   cabinet begins work on SCAP draft.

Mar. 2   cabinet completes work on "Draft for a Revised Constitution" (SCAP draft).

Mar. 4   Japanese government submits draft to SCAP. Kades and Sato with their respective teams rework the text of the draft.

Mar. 6   Japanese government announces "Outline of a Draft for a Revised Constitution." Emperor Hirohito and MacArthur give their approval.

Apr. 17   "Draft for Revised Constitution" in ordinary language announced and presented to the Privy Council.

Jun. 20   "Bill for Revision of the Imperial Constitution" submitted to the Diet.

Oct. 29   Privy Council accepts amended revision bill; it had gone back and forth between the lower and upper houses.

Nov. 3   Constitution of Japan is promulgated.

1947

May 3   Constitution of Japan comes into effect.

There are three distinct phases in the development of the Japanese Constitution; each phase has a different impact. The first phase begins with the initial efforts to revise or amend the Meiji Constitution and ends with the leak of the Matsumoto Draft (roughly from October 4, 1945 - February 1, 1946). The work was done primarily by the Japanese with minimal suggestions from American advisors. It ended in failure, but the time gap in this period allowed MacArthur to formulate his "three principles." The second phase is short and tightly condensed, starting with MacArthur's order to begin work on the draft and ending with the announcement of its completion (roughly from February 3, 1946 - February 13, 1946) in ten days. The third and final phase dates the days the SCAP draft was under consideration by the cabinet and both houses of the National Diet (roughly from February 22, 1946 - November 3, 1946), a period of a little over eight months. The time gap in this period allowed for intensive deliberations in the Diet. It was not a rush job. The Japanese officials had adequate opportunities to express their views. Whether they could have done better is debatable. Critics say under "guided democracy," with close American supervision, meaningful changes were not possible. Therefore, most observers would say the US "imposed" a constitution in Japan. While this may be substantially true, there is no denying the US did help to establish a viable constitutional democracy.

ARTICLE 9

One of the objectives of the Allied Occupation of Japan was the demilitarization of Japan. In the short term, it meant the disarming and disbanding of the military, the elimination of all means of war, the returning of military personnel from abroad, and the purging, arresting, and trying of those who were involved in war crimes. In the long term, it meant the prevention of the rise of Japanese militarism, thereby eliminating the possibility of Japan becoming a threat to the US and nearby countries.

There was a broad consensus on short-term goals, but when it came to the long-term goals, they were ambiguous and stated in broad, idealistic pronouncements. Where did such idealistic sentiments emanate from? There was a great deal of idealism and optimism in the aftermath of World War I. It was "the war to end war," and this catchphrase became popular. It turned out to be an anachronism, for it led to a bigger and more devastating war. Nevertheless, pacifism was rampant in the 1920s and culminated in the Kellogg-Briand Pact of 1928, outlawing war. The United States and France were the prime movers, and Japan was one of the signatories. It is ironic because Japan became the first nation to violate the pact when it invaded Manchuria in 1931. No actions were taken against Japan. The pact was idealistic but not realistic.

With the war raging abroad, the planners in Washington were all the more determined to prevent future wars.PWC-108b, which appeared on May 4, 1944, was written by Blakeslee and entitled, "Japan: The Postwar Objectives of the United States in Regard to Japan." He said the first objective of the US Occupation was to demilitarize Japan and the second was to prevent the return of militarism by eliminating the conditions and laws that allowed the militarists to play a large role in national politics. It was stated as follows:

> It, notwithstanding the wide consensus which now exists that Japan should not be permitted in the postwar period to retain an army, navy, or air force, Japan should later be permitted to maintain some form of military establishment, such permission should envisage as an essential condition the elimination of existing statutes and ordinances that stipulate that ministers of war and of the navy shall be high-ranking military and naval officers...[37]

Five days later, Borton, with his Quaker missionary background, made a similar argument for the abolition of Japanese militarism in PWC-152b, "Japan: Abolition of Militarism and Strengthening Democratic Processes." He argued for a thorough reform of the old political system that allowed militarism to arise.Japanese views should be respected but not at the expense of US national interest.

There was broad agreement among the planners that Japan should not have armed forces, but there was little discussion on what to do with the resulting vacuum. The key document that followed, SWNCC-228, had little to say about the consequences of demilitarization.

---

37. Notter Files, Box 142.

Since the majority of US policymakers wanted a no-war clause in the draft constitution, and it was one of the demands of FEC, MacArthur quickly decided to include the war renunciation clause. He instructed General Whitney to have the following provision (Principle II) in the draft constitution:

Principle II

War as a sovereign right of the nation is abolished. Japan renounces it as an instrumentality for settling its disputes and even for preserving its own security. It relies upon the higher ideals which are now stirring the world for its defense and its protection.

No Japanese Army, Navy, or Air Force will ever be authorized, and no rights of belligerency will ever be conferred upon any Japanese forces.[38]

Before the draft constitution was submitted to the Japanese government, MacArthur met with Prime Minister Shidehara. In their private conversation, which continued for about three hours and was not recorded, the renunciation of the war clause (later became Article 9) was discussed. It is to be noted that principle II of MacArthur's three principles cited above is similar to Article 9. A point of controversy has been the authorship of Article 9 and who had it inserted into the constitution. Shidehara claimed Article 9 was his idea, and MacArthur insisted on its inclusion in the constitution. MacArthur agreed Shidehara was the author of Article 9, and that he (MacArthur) wanted the inclusion of the clause.[39] Since there is no record of what was said and decided, the question of who was responsible for authorship and inclusion will remain problematic. But the decision was definitely made in Tokyo, not Washington, DC. The first known documented version of the no-war clause appeared in MacArthur's three principles. SWNCC had little to say about demilitarization and surely did not contemplate having a no-

---

38. SCAP, *Political Reorientation,*102 1.

39. Douglas MacArthur, *Reminiscences* (New York: Crest Books, 1964), 346-47. See Takayanagi, "Some Reminiscences," 79.

war clause in the constitution. Both MacArthur and Shidelhara were for demilitarization, MacArthur in his strong and explicit directive to Whitney, and Shidehara in his pacifist-type approach to diplomacy. When Shidehara was foreign minister in the 1920s, his cooperative-style diplomacy became known as "Shidehara diplomacy." It was noted for its policy of nonintervention and conciliatory policy, especially toward China. For both, circumstances would later force them to rationalize their position in Article 9. In MacArthur's case, the European Cold War, the Korean War, the expansion of Chinese Communism, and the increase of domestic communist and left-wing activities, made it necessary to have some kind of security force to control subversive activities. Shidehara, on the other hand, faced the same external and domestic pressures and reluctantly concluded that self-defense was needed. As part of the old guard conservative leadership, he wanted to place the onus of any move toward militarization on the Americans. If Article 9 was purely an American idea, it would make it easier to justify rearmament.

There were many questions when the draft constitution with the war renunciation clause was submitted to the Diet. A vigorous discussion ensued. Article 9, as submitted to the Diet, read as follows:

> War, as a sovereign right of the nation, and the threat or use of force, is forever renounced as a means of settling disputes with other nations.
>
> The maintenance of land, sea, and air forces, as well as other war potential, will never be authorized. The right of belligerency of the state will not be recognized.[40]

By pledging to be unarmed, isn't Japan opening itself to danger? If attacked, what about self-defense? How can Japan form alliances with other countries if it cannot fulfill its responsibilities?

At the end of the deliberations, Hitoshi Ashida, chairman of the subcommittee on constitutional revision, proposed an amendment

---

40. *https://www.ndl.go.jp* > ronten.

to Article 9. Two additional phrases were added. The following conditional phrase was added to the first paragraph, "Aspiring sincerely to an international peace based on justice and order..." And to the second paragraph, "In order to accomplish the aim of the preceding paragraph..." This second conditional phrase is referred to as the Ashida amendment. The final wording was approved by both houses of the National Diet and became the final text of Article 9 in the Japanese Constitution. It read as follows:

> Aspiring sincerely to an international peace based on justice and order, the Japanese people forever renounce war as a sovereign right of the nation and the threat or use of force as a means of settling international disputes.
>
> In order to accomplish the aim of the preceding paragraph, land, sea, and air force, as well as other war potential, will never be maintained. The right of belligerency of the state will not be recognized.

Ashida cleared with Colonel Kades and General Whitney on these changes and had their approval. At first, Ashida said that adding these two phrases made Article 9 more positive, but he soon admitted they allowed Japan to rearm. The result was ambiguity. For what purposes would you rearm? With the change, the second paragraph allows the use of self-defense to carry out the objectives of the first paragraph. Therefore, self-defense is allowed, but according to Professor Dower, there is no evidence that self-defense, as a concept, was discussed or decided on.[41] It was later that Ashida and others mentioned self-defense. Kades wrote that all nations have the inherent right of self-defense, but this writing came much later. In an interview, Kades claimed he was instructed by Whitney to draft the war renunciation clause and to do this, he relied upon the Kellogg-Briand Pact.[42] If he did write the renunciation clause, he did not include a notion of self-defense.

---

41. Dower, *Embracing*, 396.

42. Ikuhiko Hata, "Japan Under the Occupation," *The Japan Interpreter* 10, nos. 3-4 (Winter 1976): 365.

The ambiguous Ashida amendment made it possible to infer peace and order could be achieved by self-defense.

Article 9 is not long; it is succinctly written. What are the antecedents? The claim by Kades that he drew upon the Kellogg-Briand Pact is obvious when the idealistic statements in Article 9 are compared to those of the pact. Furthermore, the formulation of the phrases was guided by the following: General MacArthur's three principles, the Potsdam Declaration—the ultimatum by the United States, Great Britain, and China calling for the unconditional surrender of Japan, and the various proposals submitted by private groups and individuals. Already discussed is how PWC and SWNCC papers aided in the forming of MacArthur's three principles. These principles were further refined as they were written into Article 9. In the process of toning down phrases from these sources, they became susceptible to diverse interpretations. To sum up, starting with the bare phrases from the Kellogg-Briand Pact, MacArthur and his staff fine-tuned the article, and with the inclusion of the Ashida amendment, it remains today as Article 9 of the Japanese Constitution.

MacArthur And Yoshida

The success of occupation policies was dependent on how they were implemented, and how they were received by the Japanese people. With the Constitution in place, two individuals played critical roles in the implementation of the policies—General MacArthur and Prime Minister Yoshida.

MacArthur, with his complex personality, has been called the "benevolent despot," "American Caesar," or what the Japanese preferred, "gentle conqueror," or "American shogun" (American military ruler). Based on what he said and, in his writings, MacArthur was ethnocentric—looking down on Asians, but he could still work with the Japanese people. In contrast, the Japanese deemed MacArthur differently; he was a liberator and a savior. As a consequence of the war, the Japanese were facing poor living conditions and even starvation.

The food shortage was relieved by MacArthur's action in getting more food supplies to Japan. The general was a rescuer.[43]

Admiration of MacArthur was evident in the hundreds of thousands of letters received by SCAP. A few criticized occupation policies, but the vast majority liked what SCAP was doing and especially thanked MacArthur.[44] The Japanese became obsessed with MacArthur. He rode in a black sedan from his quarters in the American Embassy to his office in the Dai Ichi Insurance building, headquarters of SCAP. Hundreds of Japanese waited outside the building to catch a glimpse of the general as he entered the building in the morning and when he departed late in the afternoon. MacArthur worked seven days a week and kept a regular schedule. The Dai Ichi Insurance building is across the moat from the imperial place and from the general's office on the fifth floor the palace is within eyesight. The symbolism is there.

Crowd outside the Dai Ichi

43. Theodore Cohen and Herbert Passin, *Remaking Japan* (New York: The Free Press, 1987), 140.

44. Rinjiro Sodei, *Dear General MacArthur: Letters from the Japanese during the American Occupation* (Lanham, MD: Rowman & Littlefield, 2001).

MacArthur knew the emperor was important. The monarch could persuade the Japanese people to accept the occupation's policies. He could be a valuable asset for the Occupation. When Yoshida offered to arrange a meeting between the emperor and MacArthur, the general suggested they meet at his American Embassy residence. The visit was the emperor's idea and it went against tradition. The emperor received foreign dignitaries, but he never called them—this was unprecedented. MacArthur greeted the emperor and led him to a large reception room, where a military photographer was waiting. Several photos were taken. The general had planned the photo op. They then had a conversation for forty-five minutes. When the photo came out a couple of days later in the Tokyo newspapers, it created a sensation, and many Japanese were shocked.[45] Emperor Hirohito looked small and stiff in his formal morning attire, standing side by side with the tall general in his summer uniform without a tie. The photo showed the emperor to be a human being. It was clear who was the victor. By standing next to the emperor, MacArthur gained a sense of respect, the kind of respect the Japanese people gave to the emperor.

45. Finn, *Winners*, 22-24.

General MacArthur and Emperor Hirohito, Sep. 27, 1945

The photograph added to MacArthur's stature with the Japanese. MacArthur was not shy; he considered himself to be the savior of the Japanese, and he knew and exalted in the role he was playing. But he did credit Hirohito for his help in making the Occupation a success. MacArthur wanted the Occupation to end early, and he did not stay to see the official end of the Occupation. He was having increasing problems with the Truman administration, and after differences over Korean War strategies, he was recalled by President Truman. The general began preparations for the journey back to the United States. On the day he left, huge crowds of Japanese lined the streets of Tokyo, some out of curiosity, others to pay respect and to say their goodbyes to the general.

When MacArthur initially arrived in Tokyo in August 1945, he came with commanding authority and was eager to carry out his plans. This was not the case with Shigeru Yoshida. Yoshida was a career diplomat who decided to get into politics. Although he served as the Minister of Foreign Affairs in both the Higashikuni and Shidehara cabinets, he was not widely known and did not have any long-range plans. However, an opportune moment occurred when Shidehara and his cabinet resigned over an inability to carry out occupation policies. The new prime minister was supposed to be Ichiro Hatoyama, president of the Liberal Party (*Jiyuto*), but he was purged by SCAP for his wartime activities. Hatoyama asked Yoshida to be prime minister with the understanding that Hatoyama would take over once he was removed from the purge list. Yoshida reneged on this promise. Once power is tasted, it is difficult to give up.

Shigeru Yoshida
Courtesy of National Diet Library

Yoshida did not have the pedigree background of the usual leader, but he was a pragmatic politician with the ability to work with both the occupation officials and his own party politicians. He served two rounds as prime minister, making him the third-longest serving prime minister of post-occupation Japan. In the first round (1946-1947), he was responsible for enacting and implementing the many reforms of SCAP. His leadership style was bureaucratic and autocratic, and he was a confirmed conservative. The liberals in the Government Section detested Yoshida and viewed him as a reactionary. Yoshida was skeptical about SCAP reforms and moved slowly, saying the Japanese people would not accept hastily imposed policies. He was critical of constitutional revisions and almost all of the early SCAP policies. Despite his reservations, he still accepted parliamentary democracy.

Yet even with his shortcomings, he successfully worked with the Americans, mainly due to his underlying attitude. As he stated:

Being a good loser does not mean saying yes to everything the other party says, still less does it mean saying yes and going back on one's word later. It was obviously important to co-operate with the Occupation authorities to the best of one's power. But it seemed to me that where the men within GHQ were mistaken, through their ignorance of the actual facts concerned with my country, it was my duty to explain matters to them; and should their decision nevertheless be carried through, to abide by it until they themselves came to see that they had made a mistake. My policy, in other words, was to say whatever I felt needed saying, and to accept what transpired.[46]

In his second round as prime minister (1948-1954), he helped regain sovereignty for Japan. He considered the settlements resulting from the San Francisco Peace Treaty to be his greatest accomplishment. Simultaneously, a bilateral security treaty with the US was signed, allowing US military bases in Japan. For Yoshida, the US base rights were of utmost importance and by guaranteeing the security of Japan, he considered it a proud achievement.

Yoshida had a cordial relationship with MacArthur. MacArthur met with Yoshida about seventy-five times, far more than any other Japanese.[47] There is a story Yoshida told his daughter about his first meeting with MacArthur. After exchanging greetings in MacArthur's office, they talk about the emperor and how to protect the monarchy. Then, the general began to pace back and forth, giving his monologue sermon (*sekkyo* in Japanese).[48] Suddenly, Yoshida began laughing. He imagined himself locked in a cage with a pacing lion.MacArthur asked what was so funny. Yoshida answered, he thought he was hearing a lecture inside a lion's cage. MacArthur looked puzzled for a moment

---

46. Shigeru Yoshida, *The Yoshida Memoirs: The Story of Japan in Crisis*, trans. Kenichi Yoshida (Boston: Houghton Mifflin, 1962), 58-60.

47. Finn, *Winners*, 16.

48. This was a habit of MacArthur. George F. Kennan, the diplomat, related a similar experience.

and then began to laugh.[49] That is how the "ice" was broken and a friendly relationship formed.

Yoshida visits MacArthur at Waldorf-Astoria, NYC, 1954

Rarely did MacArthur meet with Japanese leaders, so his frequent meetings with Yoshida were unusual. He had few staff meetings and did not care to socialize with American officials, preferring to confide with a small circle of senior officers. MacArthur seldom left Tokyo and had no interest in Japanese culture or meeting the people. He kept to his daily routine of going from his residence to his office one mile away.

MacArthur and Yoshida were linked together by economic and security issues. They did not agree on the substance of several issues, and how to handle them, but they had a working relationship. A labor crisis loomed in early 1947 when labor unions planned a general strike by more than three million workers, beginning on the first of February. Such a strike would have severely crippled the economy and weakened the country, opening it to foreign subversion. The strike was banned by MacArthur, thus avoiding a crisis. Another issue was the increase in communist activities, both at home and abroad. When the Korean War broke out in June 1950, there was a need to have a security force to protect the Japanese people. At the insistence of MacArthur, the Yoshida

---

49. Finn, *Winners*, 23.

government established a National Police Reserve of 75,000 personnel in July 1950. It was a small step, for Yoshida resisted the pressure for a large and more rapid expansion of defense forces. Nevertheless, it was the beginning of the present-day Self-Defense Force.

Yoshida served as prime minister during the Occupation and a few years beyond. In the beginning, he was disliked by many Japanese. Disillusioned by the political leadership that had brought forth much suffering, the Japanese public was suspicious of their politicians. After his retirement, his popularity grew, and today he is considered the most prominent political leader of the early postwar period. His government began the dominant pattern of the combination of big business, bureaucracy, and the conservative political party, a triumvirate that dominated Japanese politics for decades. A nascent defense policy was established with the military and economic alliance with the US. Under Yoshida, Japan began to interpret Article 9, setting in motion the process that led to de facto rearmament.

Leadership is important, but the conditions have to be conducive for progressive provisions to take hold. The Japanese people were tired of conflict and wanted to prevent its reoccurrence by moving away from militarism. Even the political leadership took this position. Warmongering had given Japan a bad image. Asian neighbors feared the revival of a bellicose Japan, especially an emperor-centered militarism. The Japanese people and the leadership wanted the nation to play a positive role and believed Article 9 would hasten the day. Both the leaders and the people wanted Japan to be accepted in the world community and perhaps be a model.

MOVEMENTS FOR REVISION

—————————— CHAPTER THREE ——————————

Immediately after the promulgation of the 1947 Constitution of Japan, there was an outpouring of positive and negative comments about the document. It was not surprising because the content was largely new and innovative for the Japanese and was put together under special and unique circumstances. As a result, the movement for revision began, but it was sporadic and unorganized, and while the Occupation was in effect, it was inappropriate to mount a movement for revision.

The quest for change can be roughly categorized into two basic types. First, there are those who want changes made for technical and specific reasons and are pragmatically motivated. They believe if certain words or phrases are revised, it will lead to better implementation of the provision. These individuals or groups are not interested in changing whole sections of the constitution. In contrast, other individuals want total rewriting, or at least whole sections rewritten, and they want to do this for ideological and emotional reasons. This group believes the language of the 1947 Constitution does not reflect the traditions and culture of Japan, and some of the concepts are alien to the Japanese way of thinking. These two types of revisions are sometimes intertwined or blended, and when this happens, there is conflict within the revisionist groups, often resulting in a stalemate.

Opposing lines were drawn between the groups during the drafting of the constitution, its deliberation, and the beginning stages of implementation. The majority of the disagreements were along ideological lines, conservatives versus liberals or progressives. Along somewhat similar lines were the differences between traditionalists and modernists, those advocating for the old Japanese traditions and customs versus those wanting values and practices conforming to contemporary society. In addition, some insisted on the literal or strict meaning of words, while others believed in interpretation.For the textualist, every word is important in the constitution, whereas those advocating for the interpretative approach believe it is possible to achieve revision without going through the difficult phases of passing supplementary or enabling legislation.

The impetus for change was led by the political parties, principally by the Liberal Democratic Party (LDP), or *Jiminto,* which was the dominant party from its inception in 1955 until the mid-1990s. The older conservative leaders in the party such as Prime Minister Nobusuke Kishi (1957-1960) and Prime Minister Tanzan Ishibashi (1956-1957) wanted complete revision; changes were to be made in the language and stated values so they would be in line with Japanese tradition. If possible, the emperor would be more than a "symbol" of the state. In terms of Article 9, they favored rearmament, therefore, a militarization of Japan. Included in the old-line leadership were the purged politicians who could not hold political positions for a while, such as Ichiro Hatoyama (prime minister from 1954-1956) and the above-mentioned Ishibashi. Perhaps resentment over their purge led them to take on strong pro-revisionist views. However, there were those, such as Yoshida, who were not ideologically inclined and had no desire to see widespread changes. These differences among the conservative leaders impeded and slowed the revisionist movement. The major opposition parties suffered the same problems with division within their ranks. The Japan Socialist Party (JSP) or *Shakaito* and the Japan Communist Party (JCP) or *Kyosanto,* on the whole, were antirevisionists. Dissident elements within both parties made it impossible to present a united opposition to the conservatives. It is interesting to note, and somewhat ironic, that the JSP and JCP, both disdained by SCAP, turned out to be defenders of many SCAP-endorsed articles in the Constitution. Whereas, the conservative LDP, favored by the Occupation, became the leader of the movement to revise these articles.Ideological orientation caused supporters of occupation policies to be critical, and opponents to be supporters—an unusual twist in politics.

COMMISSION ON THE CONSTITUTION

No revisionist movement appeared during the Allied Occupation, but with the end of the Occupation in 1952, the conservative political parties began to agitate for revision. The two principal conservative parties merged in 1955 to form the Liberal Democratic Party (LDP). The following year, on June 11, 1956, the LDP pushed through the National Diet a law establishing the Commission on the Constitution (*Kempo chosakai*). Its purposes as stated by the enacting statute were "to examine the Constitution of Japan, to investigate and deliberate on problems related thereto and to report the results to the cabinet and through the cabinet to the National Diet." Included in its task was the investigation of the origin, performance, and all relevant issues pertaining to the constitution, and to recommend proposals for revising the constitution. The commission consisted of fifty members of whom thirty were Diet members and twenty were scholars and specialists. They were appointed by the cabinet. The commission was set up within the cabinet, but it was completely independent. Given the mission of the commission, the government wanted it to be above party politics, so the participation of the leading opposition party, the Japan Socialist Party (JSP), was requested, but the JSP declined the offer. The commission was chaired by Kenzo Takayanagi, a Harvard-trained former law professor at Tokyo University with a specialization in comparative law. He was a member of what was then the House of Peers.[50] Takayanagi was known for his impartiality.

---

50. See Robert E. Ward, "The Commission on the Constitution and Prospects for Constitutional Change in Japan." *Journal of Asian Studies*, 24 (1965): 401-29. John M. Maki, "The Documents of Japan's Commission on the Constitution." *Journal of Asian Studies*, 24 (1965): 475-89.

Prof. Kenzo Takayanagi

The commission held its first meeting on August 13, 1957, and worked for just under seven years until July 3, 1964, carrying out exhaustive investigations. Three fundamental problems relating to the Constitution of Japan were the focus of the group: (1) What kind of constitution should Japan have? (2) How should the process of the enactment of the constitution be evaluated? (3) How should the operation and the interpretation of the constitution be regarded? It gathered a variety of opinions, both for and against revision. The majority favored making several major changes. They were as follows:

- change the emperor from symbol of the state to head of state.

- change Article 9 to allow for self-defense and the maintenance of armed forces.

- reemphasize traditional family system.

- limit individual rights and freedoms where they conflict with the public interest.

- limit the rights of labor to organize and bargain.

- change some due process guarantees in criminal procedures.[51]

The commission tried to carry out impartial investigations and deliberations to avoid drifting into controversial constitutional issues, which tended to be emotional. They were not looking for comprehensive changes; most commission members favored partial and limited revisions. They wanted to stick to facts and pass on accurate information to the cabinet, the National Diet, and the public, so they could make judgments on what changes had to be made in the constitution. But as the commission did its work, it became clear there were no serious defects in the Japanese Constitution; it was working satisfactorily and there was no urgent need to revise. Moreover, the constitution enjoyed overwhelming popular support. It was obvious any serious attempt to revise it would create bitter controversy, especially with the status of the emperor and Article 9. There was even a split among the conservatives.

As a result of the upper house election in July 1956, the JSP and the other progressive parties won more than a third of the seats. The LDP did not have the necessary votes to pass a constitutional revision bill. To pass an amendment to the constitution is no easy task, for it requires a two-thirds majority of both houses of the Diet and a simple majority of a national referendum. Since it was impossible to pass a revision bill, no final recommendations were made, and consequently, no actions were taken. However, the legacy left by the commission was huge. A massive amount of data was generated and collected, cataloging every possible revision, totaling over forty thousand pages.[52]

It was understood the Commission on the Constitution would result in a largely conservative view on how to revise the Constitution, and without the participation of the JSP, it was an obvious conclusion. Some felt there was a need to counter the conservative influence of the commission. Therefore, the Constitutional Problems Study Group (*Kempo mondai kenkyukai*) was formed in 1958. It was a private organization of leading scholars of law and politics and was led by

---

51. John M. Maki, *Japan's Commission on the Constitution: The Final Report.* trans. and ed. (Seattle: University of Washington Press, 1980), 372-394.

52. This collection is of historical importance. It is the best documentary source for all aspects of the Japanese Constitution and the efforts to revise it.

Toshiyoshi Miyazawa and Hyoe Ouchi. Miyazawa, in particular, was active in the countermovement by writing papers and giving lectures. He was a constitutional scholar, and like Takayanagi, taught at Tokyo University. His conclusion that the Meiji Constitution was democratic enough and did not need to undergo extensive revisions became the principal argument used by many conservative politicians such as Joji Matsumoto; as a matter of fact, Miyazawa was a member of the Matsumoto Committee that worked on the draft rejected by SCAP. By the mid-1970s, with the Commission on the Constitution having ceased operation for over a decade and the threat of revision largely dissipated, there was little need for the group. And it disbanded in 1976.

SELF-DEFENSE FORCE

While the Commission on the Constitution was busy with its investigation, major developments occurred that had implications for Article 9. The Cold War continued to intensify, and on June 25, 1950, the Korean War began. In China, the communists had consolidated their power, while in Japan, left-wing and communist activities were on the rise. The Japanese government and SCAP recognized the immediate need to avert subversive activities.

In November 1949, the US National Security Council (NSC) authorized MacArthur to supplement the police force with a 150,000-man paramilitary police unit. The NSC made it clear this was not a move to remilitarize. Due to the sensitivity of the issue, SCAP decided to delay the implementation of the directive. MacArthur disagreed with the directive since it was questionable under the provisions of Article 9. He opposed remilitarization because the Japanese government would lose public support with such a dramatic policy shift. Prime Minister Yoshida steadfastly refused to remilitarize, citing the constitution, public opinion, and economic conditions as the reasons for his stance. However, with the outbreak of the Korean War, the situation changed drastically. American troops in Japan were diverted to South Korea to stem the North Korean invasion, thereby reducing the number of troops in Japan. Also, the intensification of left-wing demonstrations posed a problem. MacArthur sent a directive to Yoshida on July 8,

1950, authorizing the formation of the National Police Reserve (NPR) of seventy-five thousand men and an eight thousand-member Maritime Safety Agency force. Critics say the act gave rise to the revision of Article 9, but MacArthur never called for the revision of Article 9, and instead, carefully used the word "police." Even though the Yoshida government was not enthusiastic about the NPR, it nevertheless announced on August 10, 1950, the creation of the NPR. Yoshida rationalized his position by saying "forces" and "war potential" in Article 9 referred only to armed forces capable of fighting a modern war, and the NPR lacked such capabilities.[53]

At this point, Hitoshi Ashida, as chairman of an important constitutional revision committee of the lower house, wrote that the NPR was created without discussion and did not go through the legislative process. This set a bad precedent. It undermined the authority of the Diet and the will of the people as expressed in the Japanese Constitution. Furthermore, he wrote that the NPR should be considered an army.[54]

The task of the National Police Reserve was to maintain public security. SCAP assisted in its organization and equipment, and it was, in essence, a de facto military force. Still, according to the Japanese government, the NPR was not large enough to guarantee Japan's security needs. Shortly thereafter, the security arrangement changed radically when Japan regained its sovereignty with the signing of the San Francisco Peace Treaty on September 8, 1951. On the same day, the Mutual Security Treaty between Japan and the US was signed, assuring Japan that the US would come to its defense if attacked. It allowed the Americans to have military bases in Japan and to station its personnel. Meanwhile, on October 15, 1952, the NPR was expanded to 110,000 personnel and renamed the National Safety Force (NSF). A big gap in the security needs of Japan was filled.

The next major step in the reorganization came on July 1, 1954, when the Defense Agency was established, and the National Safety Force was reorganized as the Self-Defense Force (SDF) or *Jieitai*. The

---

53. Haruhiro Fukui, "Twenty Years of Revisionism," in Henderson, *The Constitution of Japan*, 56-57.

54. *https://www.ndl.go.jp* > description 13.

SDF is composed of three branches: the Ground Self-Defense Force (GSDF), which is the present-day army; the Maritime Self-Defense Force (MSDF), which is the present-day navy; and the Air Self-Defense Force (ASDF), which is the present-day air force. Of course, this is misleading terminology. The Japanese government was forced to use nondescript words to describe its military forces because Article 9 forbids Japan from having an armed force. Make no mistake, the SDF is a modern, sophisticated military force, equipped with the latest weapons, increasing its capability to undertake offensive missions.[55]

The final transition came fifty-three years later, on January 9, 2007, when the Ministry of Defense was created. This is a cabinet ministry and is equivalent to the US Department of Defense.[56] It took a long time for institutionalized militarism to take hold, and the delay was due, in large part, to the persistent anti-militaristic attitude prevalent in Japan.

In the view of the Japanese government, these developments are not in violation of Article 9; therefore, they are constitutional. According to the government, Japan has the "inherent" right of self-defense and is justified in creating the SDF. Article 9 does not prohibit military forces for purposes of defense. Japan is a member of the United Nations, and Article 51 of the United Nations Charter recognizes "the inherent right of individual or collective self-defense." Furthermore, the San Francisco Peace Treaty states, "Japan as a sovereign nation possesses the inherent right of individual or collective self-defense." On the other hand, the opposition does not recognize the right of self-defense and believes the SDF to be unconstitutional. Nevertheless, the SDF has won general acceptance from the Japanese public. Polls showed more people wanted to strengthen defenses than weaken them.

---

55. The use of unobtrusive terms abounds. What is called "ordinary units" are infantry units and what is called "escort ships" includes a whole range of ships, like the 26,000-ton Izumo-class helicopter destroyers, two of which are being modified as light aircraft carriers. They are still classified as destroyers because Japan is not supposed have "offensive" vessels. Other nations use unobtrusive terms. Israel's armed forces is called the IDF (Israel Defense Force).

56. *https://www.mod.go.jp* > w_paper. This source is the Annual White Paper, which is in digest and full versions. It is a comprehensive record of the functions and activities of the Ministry of Defense.

Has the constitutional legality of the SDF been challenged? Doesn't the stationing of US forces in Japan under arrangements of a security treaty create a "war potential," thereby violating Article 9? Judicial review is the power of the courts to determine the constitutionality of the acts of the legislative and executive branches of the government. It is to help preserve the separation of powers between the legislative, executive, and judicial branches. Judicial review does this and is a powerful procedure in several Western democracies. But in Japan, it was new and inserted into the constitution by the American occupiers as Article 81—"The Supreme Court is the court of last resort with power to determine the constitutionality of any law, order, regulation or official act." Over the years, cases of judicial review have been infrequent in the Japanese Supreme Court.

The first Supreme Court case dealing with Japan's defense policies was the 1959 *Sunakawa* case (*Sakata v. Japan*). A group of farmers were facing the confiscation of their land and eviction because of the proposed extension of the runway at the US Tachikawa base. The extension would run into the neighboring village of Sunakawa. The farmers' protest soon broadened into a nationwide protest that became part of the antibase movement. University student activists, known as *Zengakuren* (League of Student Associations), labor unions, and Japan Socialist Party members all joined in the protest. It was said to be a protest protecting the "Peace Constitution" from "American imperialism."[57]

Specifically, the case involved seven protestors who were arrested for trespassing by forcefully entering the base. On March 30, 1959, the Tokyo District Court made the dramatic decision that the SDF, the Mutual Security Treaty, and the stationing of US forces in Japan were in violation of the war renunciation clause of the Japanese Constitution and were, therefore, unconstitutional. The court said using private land for military purposes is in violation of Article 9. The seven protestors were exonerated. This lower court decision caused an uproar in Japan and the US. The decision was quickly appealed. The Japanese Supreme

---

57. For documentation of the *Sunakawa* case, see John M. Maki, *Court and Constitution in Japan: Selected Supreme Court Decisions, 1948-60* (Seattle: University of Washington Press, 1964), 298-361.

Court in 1959 overturned the lower court and ruled the SDF, the security treaty, and the US bases in Japan were constitutional and not in violation of Article 9. The seven protesters were found not guilty of trespassing. Protests continued and the runway extension was eventually dropped. Years later, declassified US documents revealed Supreme Court Justice Kotaro Tanaka had discussed the case with the US Embassy before the ruling, and it is alleged Tanaka tried to persuade other justices. This incident seriously undermined judicial independence. It is interesting to note that the Supreme Court was careful and did not consider the constitutionality of Article 9 itself. It only ruled on the constitutionality of the US military bases in Japan, the accompanying security treaty, and the SDF. The justices felt Article 9 was too big a political issue and should be handled by the National Diet and the cabinet, and it was not a purview of the court. Still, even with this limitation, the *Sunakawa* ruling has influenced cases related to military bases, for example, citizens challenging private land used for military purposes in Okinawa.

The *Naganuma Nike Missile Site* case is another case with a similar outcome. On September 7, 1973, the Sapporo District Court held that the SDF violated Article 9, which prohibits armed forces and the maintenance of "war potential." The Air Self-Defense Force wanted to construct a Nike missile base in a forest preserve. Residents protested that this was a protected forest reserve and served as an essential watershed, providing fresh water and flood control. They argued the people had a "right to live in peace." The Sapporo High Court and later the Supreme Court in 1982 reversed the lower-court decision because the base was already built, conditions had changed, and alternative facilities had resolved the problems. Therefore, the plaintiffs lost standing. The court refused to rule on the constitutionality of the SDF, nor did it mention the people's right to live in peace.

Ever since the Self-Defense Force was formed, the Japanese Supreme Court has defended the actions of the government, ruling that the SDF, the treaty arrangements, the establishment of bases, and the employment of defensive weapons, are all constitutional and not in violation of Article 9.[58] Under the guise of Article 9, the court has approved the incremental expansion of SDF activities. However, the court has avoided ruling on the constitutionality of Article 9 itself by using the doctrine of "political question," that is, the issue is too political and should be handled by the legislative and executive branches.

It was not through judicial decisions but through executive actions that the role of the SDF was expanded. A major policy move was the National Defense Program Guidelines (NDPG) adopted by the Cabinet and the National Defense Council in October 1976. The guidelines set forth Japan's defense capabilities, the roles of the defense forces, and the deployment and maintenance of personnel and equipment. It is the first statement on how US and Japanese forces would work together. The outline includes the SDF response to domestic and international natural disaster relief and its contribution to international peacekeeping missions. The NDPG's stated objective, in part, is as follows:

> The most consequential responsibility of the Government of Japan is to maintain Japan's peace and security, to ensure its survival and to defend to the end Japanese nationals' life, person and property of its nationals and territorial land, waters, and airspace...Carrying out this responsibility by exerting efforts on its own accord and initiative is at the very heart of Japan's national security. Japan's defense capability is the ultimate guarantor of its security and the clear representation of the unwavering will and ability of Japan as a peace-loving nation.[59]

---

58. In the *Eniwa* case (*Japan v. Nozaki Bros.*) of 1967, the Supreme Court upheld the government action in arresting the two brothers for cutting the phone lines of the SDF, although they were acquitted on technicalities. The court avoided ruling on the constitutionality of Article 9, following the differential approach of avoiding "political questions." Similarly, in the *Hyakuri Air Base* case (1989), the court ruled SDF was constitutional, but refrained from ruling on Article 9, citing the "political question" theory.

59. *https://www.cas.go.jp* > pdf.

DEPARTURE FROM RELATIVE ISOLATIONISM

The Gulf War of 1990-91 was a pivotal event for Japan's defense policy. It was a military campaign led by the United States in a thirty-nine-nation coalition against Saddam Hussein's Iraq in retaliation for invading Kuwait. Japan was asked to join the coalition. Since Japan is a close mutual security treaty partner, it felt obligated to contribute. But Japan balked at sending armed military personnel due to constitutional restraints and eventually contributed $13 billion. Heavy criticism was leveled at Japan by coalition members for buying its way out with money instead of sending military personnel. American officials said it was "checkbook diplomacy." The Japanese government was embarrassed, and SDF officials felt humiliated.

The following year, the Diet passed the Peacekeeping Operations Act in reaction to the humiliation it suffered in 1991. It was not an easy task to pass the bill because the Japan Socialist Party employed, as one of its obstructionist tactics, the unique Japanese form of filibuster called "ox walk," where Diet members slowly walked to cast their votes. The bill eventually passed, and the JSP suffered a setback in the next election because of its delaying tactics. The SDF could now be deployed in overseas operations.

There are two types of peacekeeping operations (PKO) utilizing military personnel. One would be the United Nations Peacekeeping Operations (UNPKO) in noncombat zones. The other would be coalition-led operations in combat zones. In the first type, PKO under the auspices of the UN is used in a wide variety of activities, including natural disaster relief resulting from earthquakes, wildfires, floods, tsunamis, hurricanes, and so forth, and humanitarian relief, covering hunger, medical aid and assistance to refugees. Transportation is another vital need that is provided for the distribution of food, water, and other supplies. In addition, troops help with road repairs and the reconstruction of facilities and are used as cease-fire and truce observers. These are all noncombat activities. In the second type, soldiers of the coalition forces are used to enforce or maintain peace and order in combat zones. They prevent terrorists and rebel groups from gaining a foothold, or they may help maintain an existing truce or cease-fire. Furthermore, they assist the established government by providing protection and supplying transportation and other logistical support.

After the passage of the Peacekeeping Operations Act in 1992, Japan sent its first unit under the United Nation's UNPKO to Cambodia. For one year, a six hundred men SDF engineer unit provided transportation for food and water and acted as truce observers. What followed were over a dozen UNPKO missions with SDF personnel deployed in Mozambique, Rwanda, Golan Heights (Israel, Syria), Honduras, Turkey, Timor-Leste, India, Haiti, East Timor, Iran, Thailand, Indonesia, Nepal, Pakistan, New Zealand, and South Sudan. Besides ground troops, naval vessels were employed in anti-piracy operations for several years in the Gulf of Aden (Somalia). These UNPKO missions required substantial financial support. Japan ranks third, following the US and China, in the financial contributions made to UNPKO.

External events can profoundly impact the interpretation and implementation of Article 9. Immediately after al-Qaeda's terrorist attacks on the World Trade Center and the Pentagon on September 11, 2001, Prime Minister Koizumi called President George W. Bush and offered assistance. Bush decided to declare a "war on terror" and began plans for an international antiterrorism coalition against al-Qaeda. Japan took immediate steps with the Diet passing the Antiterrorism Special Measures Law on October 29, 2001. It was Japan's contribution to the global war on terrorism. By this law, the SDF is given authority to cooperate and support activities with the US, but it is limited to noncombative roles such as search and rescue operations and providing aid and humanitarian services. In Afghanistan, the support was in the transportation of supplies, the handling of refugees, and economic aid for rehabilitation purposes.

In addition, the Maritime Self-Defense Force (MSDF) was used to provide logistical support for the US-led air and naval antiterrorism coalition in the Indian Ocean. MSDF vessels were used to refuel ships from other countries, and this took place for about eight years. Media coverage of this noncombat role gave the SDF a good image.[60]

Good image, however, was lacking in the next big step the Japanese government took in the Middle East. The US-led coalition attacked Iraq on March 20, 2003. The justification given was that Iraq under Saddam Hussein was alleged to have manufactured and stored weapons of mass destruction and was actively supporting terrorist groups, including al-Qaeda. Koizumi had promised to support the US in the Middle East, and he now pushed for legislation to authorize the deployment of SDF personnel to Iraq. The decision was made to shift from noncombat UNPKO missions to a US-led coalition engaged in combatting insurgency. There was fierce opposition, but Koizumi persisted, and the bill passed. Polls showed more than half of the voters were opposed to the legislation. Opposition was so widespread that it resulted in twelve lawsuits filed in eleven cities. The argument most frequently used in the lawsuits was that the citizens' "right to live in peace" shall not be jeopardized by the overseas deployment of troops. It was the argument used by the plaintiffs in the *Naganuma Nike Missile Site* case. The lawsuits were dismissed, and no appeals were made to the Supreme Court. The legal process was lengthy and rendered moot by the end of the deployment. The plaintiffs were satisfied they had made their point—citizens have the "right to live in peace" from Japan's participation in a war abroad.[61]

On January 4, 2004, about 5,500 GSDF personnel, mostly military engineers, were sent to Iraq. It was a multilateral military mission outside of UNPKO and was the largest deployment of Japanese troops since World War II. Once the troops arrived, stationing them was a problem. They were supposed to be in a noncombat zone, but in Iraq,

---

60. The resources of the SDF were not immediately utilized in the Great Hanshin Earthquake of 1995. The delay was partly due to the negative attitude held by public and local officials toward the SDF. Nevertheless, the SDF assisted in search and rescue, reconstruction, and in the transportation and distribution of supplies. Fifty-six years later, the attitude toward the SDF had completely changed. The government immediately ordered the mobilization of one hundred thousand SDF personnel to assist in the Fukushima nuclear disaster of 2011.

61. Tomoyuki Sasaki, "Whose Peace? Anti-Military Litigation and the Right to Live in Peace in Postwar Japan," *The Asia-Pacific Journal: Japan Focus*, 10, issue 29, no. 1 (July 9, 2012): 14-15.

there were few "safe" zones. Rebel units were scattered throughout Iraq. A "safe" zone was finally found in the city of Samawah. The GSDF unit was there for two and a half years, providing water and health services, transportation needs, and rebuilding public infrastructure. Unfortunately, fighting broke out around Samawah, and the GSDF detachment had to be in lockdown. They were no longer able to carry on their work. Samawah had become a "war zone." In modern warfare, often there is no "front line" with violence happening all over. Improvised explosive devices (IEDs) or homemade bombs are used in unconventional ways, such as booby traps, ambushes and other tactics of guerrilla warfare. In addition, the use of long-range missiles blurred the distinction between combat and noncombat zones. Military experts say it is folly to send unarmed personnel into a combat zone. You cannot depend on others to protect you. The lesson is obvious— military deployment to a combat zone cannot succeed without the option of using reasonable military force.

The situation quickly escalated when four Japanese civilians were kidnapped by a rebel group. Three were eventually released, but one was beheaded. The SDF in Iraq did not suffer any casualties and was brought home in July 2006. The mission was deemed a failure, and Koizumi was severely criticized for sending the SDF into a dangerous situation. His popularity dropped, and the political cost was heavy.

What has taken place since the 1990s is a gradual move away from relative isolationism and pacifism towards an active international role. Pacifist principles enshrined in Article 9 were gradually eroded by de facto rearmament. Japan never was and never will be a pacifist state. Pacifism abhors the use of military force. However, Japan supported the use of military force by the US in the Gulf War and Afghanistan. Granted, the missions undertaken by the SDF have been noncombat roles, but recent military operations have blurred the distinction between noncombative and combative. With the acquisition of new offensive capabilities, will Japan be willing to use coercive action in a situation where it has legitimate reasons? Japan is willing to contribute to international security. These are actions taken or supported by the conservative government. What is lacking is broad popular support.

LDP DRAFT OF 2005

After a lull of about forty-five years, the LDP and right-wing circles began to seriously push for constitutional revision. The move for constitutional revision had been building up in the 1990s. As previously discussed, when Japan was called to make military contributions to the resolution of the Gulf War of 1990-91, it was slow to respond, and when action was finally taken, only financial aid was offered with no military personnel or equipment. LDP leaders wanted to rectify the situation.

In January 2000, Constitutional Research Councils were set up in both the House of Representatives and the House of Councillors of the National Diet. The purpose of the two multiparty councils was to promote debate and make recommendations, especially regarding Article 9. It was primarily motivated by a desire to see Japan as a world leader. The conservatives viewed a strong Japan as being less dependent on its ally, the United States, and playing a major role in world politics. To achieve this vision, it became necessary to revise or eliminate some provisions of the constitution so it would meet the needs of the Japanese people and respond to the challenges of present-day Japan. In August 2005, Prime Minister Junichiro Koizumi announced a plan to create a draft constitution. He was prime minister from 2001 to 2006, and as prime minister, he was automatically the leader of the LDP. Koizumi enjoyed wide popular support but was seen as a maverick leader of the LDP and somewhat flamboyant. After the councils of both chambers submitted their report and the Democratic Party of Japan (DPJ), or *Minshuto,* affirmed its support, Koizumi decided to move aggressively for a draft constitution.

Junichiro Koizumi
Courtesy of Cabinet Public Affairs Office

The draft was published on November 22 by the LDP. Several proposals followed the suggestions made by the Commission on the Constitution. The major changes made by the draft provisions were as follows:

- completely rewrote the preamble.
- changed Article 9 by permitting a "defense force" and use of the term "*gun*" (army or military).
- added military courts to Article 76.
- softened wording in Article 13 regarding respect for individual rights.
- permitted state funding of religious institutions under Article 89.
- changed Articles 92 and 95 concerning local self-government and relations between local and national governments.

- changed Article 96 requiring only a simple majority to pass an amendment but retaining the national referendum.

The following should be noted for their wide implications: (1) by inserting new words, for example, *"gun"* for "army or military" the existence of the Self-Defense Force is justified and, therefore, constitutional; (2) the addition of military courts solidifies the claim that Japan does have military forces; and (3) by having a simple majority vote in both the lower and upper houses of the Diet, a formidable obstacle in passing any constitutional amendment is eliminated. These changes would have been a major revision of the Japanese Constitution.

Outside right-wing groups joined with the LDP in a drive to pass the constitutional draft of 2005. They were strongly opposed by diverse interest groups who found they could unite in a common cause. Meanwhile, the LDP was no longer the dominant ruling party in the Diet and needed the support of some minor parties. The leading minor party, the Clean Government Party (CGP), or *Komeito,* agreed with most of the proposals, but when it came to Article 9, it adamantly opposed the change. The LDP could not count on the CGP support. The Democratic Party of Japan (DPJ), or *Minshuto,* was the only party to join, but it was insufficient. The LDP simply did not have the required two-thirds vote in both houses to amend the constitution. Thus, their effort to implement a draft constitution came to naught.

DRAFT OF 2012

Seven years had passed since the LDP attempted to pass a draft constitution. During this interim period, the dispute over revision continued with occasional inflammatory utterances by politicians making headlines. Nationalistic pronouncements by right-wing elements were especially provocative. The possibility for some kind of revision of the constitution seemed brighter in 2007 when a coalition of the LDP and CGP passed a bill in both houses of the Diet, which created detailed procedures for holding a national referendum. This made it clear what needed to be done at the national level with the voters. But there was still the requirement of a two-thirds vote to pass a constitutional amendment bill in both houses of the Diet. Alas, the coalition lacked the two-thirds votes in the upper house.

Nevertheless, on May 7, 2012, the LDP decided to issue a new draft constitution. A booklet designed to educate the public about the draft constitution summarized it in an effort "to make the Constitution more suitable for Japan." To a large degree, the draft is similar to that of 2005. This new draft has eleven chapters comprising 110 articles, whereas the 1947 Constitution has ten chapters with 103 articles. Here are the main points of the 2012 draft:

- complete redrafting of the preamble.
- prescriptions on the use of the national flag and the national anthem.
- emperor is head and symbol of the State.
- prescriptions on the right of self-defense and Defense Forces.
- maintains pacifism.
- balances personal rights and freedom with more emphasis on the responsibilities and duties of citizens in "maintaining public order."
- new chapter on state of emergency.
- provides for procedures to amend constitution.

The right of self-defense is justified by calling for the defense of the nation's territory with a "National Defense Force." This change is a matter of semantics, replacing a word ("self") with a new one ("national") to give the appearance of a new approach. More important is the introduction of the "doctrine of collective self-defense," where Japan would play a role in international peacekeeping and be a partner in collective security alliances. Japan would come to the aid of any ally being attacked, and in turn, alliance members would come to its defense if attacked. Japan is to be an active player in international politics.

But first and foremost was the need to change Article 96, the amendment clause, the last item listed above. When Shinzo Abe became President of the LDP and Prime Minister of Japan for the second time in December 2012, he pointed to Article 96 as the critical revision. The amendment hurdle is too difficult for the LDP to overcome, requiring a two-thirds majority in both houses. From the 1960s to the 1980s, the LDP dominated the political scene, and Japan was said to have a "one-and-one-half-party system," where the LDP was the "one" and all the rest of the opposition parties combined were the "one-half." It is also referred to as the "1955 system" since the LDP was formed in 1955 in response to the unification of the socialist parties. Even with this dominance, nothing was done about constitutional revision because the factions in the LDP were not in agreement, and the party lacked popular support. By the 1990s, the LDP lost its dominance and needed the help of the smaller parties. Although the LDP was able to form a coalition with such small parties as the DPJ and the Japan Innovation Party (JIP) or *Nippon Ishin no Kai*, it lacked the full support of a key coalition member, the CGP or *Komeito*. At the time, CGP had thirty-one votes in the lower house. On most matters, *Komeito* worked closely with the LDP, but with Article 9 the party was opposed to armed intervention. *Komeito's* opposition to this single aspect of Article 9 meant an end to the efforts of a revision. CGP was founded in 1964 by members of *Soka Gakkai,* a lay Buddhist movement. In line with its religious beginning, the influence of pacifist views was heavy. This accounts for its strong opposition to any attempt to tamper with Article 9. Minor parties had different agendas, so it was difficult to form a cohesive coalition, especially on a highly controversial issue like Article 9. In 2012, the LDP draft constitution tried to overcome this obstacle with its revised amendment procedure.

Shinzo Abe

Given the lack of votes to pass any significant constitutional revision measures in the Diet, Prime Minister Abe decided to focus the attention of the LDP on a single approach to Article 9—to reinterpret it. Abe believed Article 9 was the key to Japan regaining its status as a major actor in world politics. It is a matter of national prestige, and the nationalistic right wing of the LDP is passionate and vocal about recovering Japan's honor.

Meanwhile, the security environment in Asia changed with China exerting increased pressure, necessitating the need for security cooperation with the United States and other allies in the region to protect the Japanese people. To meet this challenge, changes had to be made to Article 9 by reinterpretation, and this was to be done by executive action.

The strategy to reinterpret Article 9 is called the "right of collective self-defense." Abe decided to temporarily bypass the Diet and a national referendum. Instead, he used the Cabinet Legislative Bureau to reinterpret Article 9. On July 1, 2014, the cabinet approved the reinterpretation of Article 9 following an agreement between the ruling

LDP and its junior coalition partner CGP. It was carefully worded and limited to certain cases. Japan will be allowed to exercise the right of self-defense under three conditions. First, when a nation with close ties to Japan comes under attack and the lives of Japanese nationals are clearly endangered. Second, that force may be used only if there is no other effective way to protect the lives of Japanese citizens. Finally, the use of force is to be limited to a minimally required level.

The reinterpretation allows the SDF, under certain conditions, to come to the aid of an allied nation that is under attack. Japan itself does not need to be attacked. The SDF can work with the US under the Security Treaty arrangement and allied partners in the "immediate vicinity of Japan." SDF would be allowed in certain situations to provide logistical support to foreign militaries in noncombat zones. And the SDF would continue to participate in United Nations peacekeeping operations.

In reaction to this new approach, there were large protest demonstrations throughout the country. Critics viewed Abe's strategy as a backhanded way to revise Article 9 and perhaps even the entire constitution. They said any changes to the constitution should be made through the Diet and by public referendum, not by a cabinet reinterpretation. *Komeito,* the leading coalition partner, decided to pull away and opposed the reinterpretation. Furthermore, public opinion polls continued to show over two-thirds of the populace supported the "Peace Constitution" and were concerned about the trend towards increasing militarism in Japan. Due to the intense opposition to the collective self-defense reinterpretation, the LDP could not move forward on the rest of the 2012 draft constitution. In addition, internal party strife and coalition struggles, plus serious economic issues, all combined and led to the failure of the draft constitutional reform.

PROSPECT

The focus has been on the status of the emperor and Article 9, but they are only two of the myriad of occupation policies. The other programs, in their successes or failures, undoubtedly had an impact on the two issues chosen for this study. For example, the constitutional articles on individual rights and responsibilities and labor rights were enthusiastically supported by the public. Along with the articles on the emperor system and Article 9, they were part and parcel of the 1947 Constitution, and as a complete package have been favorably supported by the Japanese people. Therefore, there was some spillover support for the emperor and Article 9. But even a highly successful reform, like the one on individual rights and responsibilities, had detractors who wanted to tone it down and make other adjustments, as seen in the LDP drafts of 2005 and 2012. Regardless, the vested interest in defending these rights was so strong that the chance of making changes was remote. Strong support from the people in how they embraced a policy determined its fate—whether it was accepted, rejected, or modified. Reforms on education and local government had few supporters. At the end of the Occupation, the Japanese abandoned or changed these policies and essentially returned to their traditional ways. Hence, whether a policy would be kept, with or without changes, depends on the degree of support it receives from the people and the leadership.

Changes in the international environment and domestic scene can affect revisionism. The rise of Chinese Communism in East Asia, the Cold War, and the increase in communist activities domestically caused the Occupation to shift from an economic reform policy to a program for economic recovery. Beginning in 1947, there was a complete reversal in occupation policies—from policies dismantling the economy so it would never again support war machinery to policies hastening the economic recovery so Japan could defend itself against communist subversion or outside attacks. This was part of the so-called "reverse course." Such external events and internal political developments directly impacted the prospects for reform.

With these considerations in mind, what are the prospects for change in the role of the emperor and the imperial institution? The uniqueness of the Japanese imperial institution has raised many questions about its future. Even at the height of the Japanese prewar liberalism of the 1920s, some doubted the compatibility of the imperial system with democracy, and these thoughts had to be countered. Sakuzo Yoshino, a professor of political history and theory, wrote the following:

First, there is absolutely no contradiction nowadays between the "interest of the Imperial Family" and the interest of the nation, [an interest] which stands at the very top of the people's well-being...Since the Imperial Family is the unique head of the national family, it is utterly unthinkable that it should become necessary "in the interest of the Imperial Family" to disregard the interest of the people. Consequently, I believe the interest of the Imperial Family and the interest of the people can never conflict with each other.[62]

For Professor Yoshino, the emperor system and democracy could coexist, and there was no need for drastic reforms. Even though many American prewar and postwar planners were in favor of retaining the emperor and the imperial system, it was not a consensus; there were sharp criticisms. The controversy has continued to this day. Nevertheless, the majority of Japanese people approve of the imperial system. Public opinion polls have consistently shown support without much fluctuation. A distinct minority of right-wing nationalistic activists would like to add the words "head of state" to go along with "symbol of state" and the concept of *kokutai* (usually translated as "national unity"), essentially returning the locus of sovereignty to the emperor. Japan would be a unique nation, one of its kind, with the longest continuous reign in the world. The country would be one big family with the emperor as the father and the people as his children. Most Japanese today would not relate to *kokutai.* Popular sovereignty, where people are the source of governmental power, has become a bedrock principle. One could argue for minor changes in the language and the use of specific words to reflect Japanese traditions and thinking. But there is little appetite for even cosmetic changes because it could open the gate to major changes that would have severe consequences.

What is troublesome for critics of the imperial system is the possibility of subverting a constitutional monarchy by shifting towards an imperial monarchy, where the emperor is allowed to make political decisions or be used to legitimize the use of military force. It happened

---

62. Wm. Theodore de Bary, ed. *Sources of Japanese Tradition* (New York: Columbia University Press, 1958), 732.

in the 1930s and 1940s. Documents reveal how Emperor Hirohito stubbornly resisted surrendering when he knew defeat was inevitable, causing the death of hundreds of thousands of civilians in the Battle of Okinawa and the atomic bombings.

The postwar public acceptance of the emperor and his family is largely due to their behavior and performance. When Emperor Hirohito renounced his "divinity" over the radio on January 1, 1946, it shocked the nation. This was the first time most Japanese citizens heard his voice. He spoke in a colloquial style instead of the formalistic style barely understandable by most Japanese. The Japanese people did not use his name Hirohito. He was known to his subjects as *Showa-tenno* (*Showa* Emperor). *Showa* is the name of the emperor's reign.

Somehow, the divine aura of the emperor had to be dispelled. He had to show he was not godlike. It was decided that Emperor Hirohito would tour the country and speak with the people, but it must have been a difficult decision because he was known to have little regard for the Japanese people. In a secret document discovered in 1999, the Emperor's views are stated:

> …The Emperor felt that there were still many remnants of feudalism in the Japanese mind and that it would take a long time to eradicate them. He said the Japanese people as a whole were lacking in education which was necessary for their democratization and also that they were lacking in real religious feeling and were accordingly easy to sway from one extreme to the other. He said that one of the feudalistic traits was their willingness to be led and that they were not trained like Americans to think for tthemselves.[63]

---

63. Axel Berkofsky, *A Pacifist Constitution for an Armed Empire: Past and Present of Japanese Security and Defence Policies* (Milan: Franco Angeli, 2012), 49.

Beginning of Emperor Hirohito's nationwide tour, Feb. 1946

The imperial tours began on February 19, 1946, and were unprecedented. In prewar days, people never viewed the emperor, and if he passed by in a procession, their heads were bowed, so they never laid eyes on him. To see the emperor close-up was an unusual experience. Within two years, Emperor Hirohito visited every prefecture, except Okinawa, traveling some 20,500 miles.

Another event that sent shock waves throughout the country was the previously discussed photograph taken on September 27, 1945, with Emperor Hirohito, attired in a formal morning coat, standing next to General MacArthur, casually dressed in his summer uniform. It showed who was in charge and that the emperor was certainly not a divine figure. These activities made the emperor relatable. The successors to Emperor Hirohito, Emperors Akihito and Naruhito, have carried out their duties to fulfill Article 1, that the emperor shall be the "unity of the people." The royal family performed their ceremonial duties without fanfare and lived rather austere lives without scandals. They cannot interfere with politics, and their comments are vetted. The British royal family, in contrast, have been involved in scandals and seemingly take part in ceremonial events to display the latest fashion. Ostentatious living does not engender public support. The imperial family has avoided such criticisms and has the approval of the vast majority in postwar Japan.

An indication of the support for the imperial family and tradition was the Japanese government's decision in 1946 to retain the traditional way of counting the years. Each time a different emperor begins to rule, a new counting of the years commences, and the period acquires a new name. The year is indicated first by the reign name, followed by the number of years since the start of the reign. For example, 1946 is *Showa* 21. *Showa* is the reign name for Emperor Hirohito, and it is followed by the number of years since the reign. In the long run, there will always be questions about why an anachronistic institution exists within a progressive, fast-moving society. Revisionists believe changes in the imperial system will strengthen Japan, but it could, in fact, seriously damage the social and political fabric of Japan. It is an emotional issue because it touches on the essence of modern Japan.

When it comes to Article 9, it is a different story. Changes have been made and will continue to be made. However, it is not through changes in the text but through interpretations. A whole set of words have arisen to describe the process. It has been called the "revision of the reinterpretation," "creeping constitutionality," "linguistic gymnastics," and other descriptive terms.

These incremental changes were tolerated by the public. The SDF received high marks for its relief work during the 2011 Fukushima earthquake and tsunami disaster and for its other disaster-relief missions. But when it comes to missions involving the possible use of force, even in self-defense, a strong emotional response is aroused. And there is the perception that Japanese participation in missions involving the use of force is due to US pressure. It seems ambivalent, but the Japanese public favors the use of the SDF for relief and humanitarian purposes, and at the same time, abhors its use in any situation involving combat, even for a good cause.

During the premiership of Shinzo Abe, a concerted effort was initiated to legitimize and increase the stature of the SDF and to expand its role. He served as prime minister from 2006-7 and 2012-20, the longest tenure in postwar Japan. In September 2020, Abe resigned his premiership for health reasons and was not able to accomplish his major goal of revising Article 9. Intra-party disputes, disagreements with coalition partners, plus political scandals derailed any efforts to pass reforms. Out of office, he continued to advocate for the revision of Article 9. In July 2022, while campaigning in Nara for an LDP candidate in the House of Councilors election, he was shockingly assassinated.

The assassination restarted the debate about amending the constitution. Prime Minister Fumio Kishida and the LDP vowed to continue the movement to honor Abe's legacy. But the same challenges persist. After the July House of Councilors election, the pro-revisionists increased to 62 percent of the chamber. When the question was narrowed to the specific issue of SDF's capabilities, or giving it legal status, the support was even greater. The LDP needed the support of the minor parties and needed to form a coalition to pass any legislation in the lower and upper houses. Its coalition partners are the CGP, JIP, and the Democratic Party for the People (DPP) or *Kokumin Minshuto*. The CGP is the junior partner with the largest number of seats among the smaller parties, but barely half of them support any kind of constitutional revision. And when it comes to Article 9, the support is even weaker. Herein lies the problem for the LDP—it cannot rely on the CGP to pass any revision or addition to Article 9.

Although domestic developments play a large role in motivating a revision of Article 9, the evolving international environment could arouse greater anxieties that lead to changes. Prime Minister Fumio Kishida's government has proposed to move from a strictly defense-oriented policy (*senshu boei*) to one of power projected beyond its borders, with the capability to strike military targets in the enemy's territory. This sounds like an offensive strategy, and again semantics is involved, but technological advancements have made the distinction between defense and offensive capabilities more difficult. It has blurred this vital part of Japan's defense policy. For example, defensive missiles designed to destroy incoming missiles, drones, and aircraft, can be used for offensive purposes. Drones that were developed for reconnaissance and surveillance purposes are now fitted with bombs and used offensively. Both the Ukrainians and Russians have demonstrated how defensive weapons are implemented for offensive purposes in the Ukraine War.

China poses security challenges with its rapidly expanding military power. Deployment of its forces includes long-range and hypersonic missiles, sophisticated jet fighters, and new naval warships, such as aircraft carriers. The ownership of the Senkaku Islands has been challenged by China, and there has been an increase in Chinese naval and air traffic in the vicinity of the islands. Nearby is Taiwan, where Chinese air and naval activities have intensified with a hint of possible invasion.Meanwhile, North Korea is testing long-range missiles and has developed a nuclear arsenal. Some of the missiles have flown over Japan. Adding to the anxiety is Russia's invasion of Ukraine, which revived the dispute with Russia over parts of the Kuril Islands. There is an increase in Russian military activities near northern Japan, and joint military exercises with China have been held in this area.

To counter the expanding momentum of China and North Korea, the capabilities of the SDF have been increased and are reflected in recent defense spending. For over five decades, starting from the 1960s, military spending was at or below one percent of GDP. It is remarkable that Japan was able to maintain a steady level of defense spending over a long period. There was no sharp increase or decrease in the defense budget. This is all the more notable for a budget that ranks at the top level of the world's leading defense budgets. Because Japan's GDP is huge, even one percent is a large amount for defense spending. According to the Stockholm International Peace Research Institute (SIPRI), Japan was the tenth-largest defense spender in the world in 2022.Japan spent $46 billion (6 trillion yen), but despite a budget increase, fell one notch from ninth to tenth, right below South Korea. Japan's military budget was 1.08 percent of GDP.[64]

In the midst of a deteriorating regional security environment, on December 16, 2022, the Japanese government announced a new security strategy and defense plans. The first security strategy was approved in

---

64. Diego Lopes da Silva, Xiao Jiang, Lorenzo Scarazzato, Lucie Beraud-Sudreau, Ana Assis, and Nan Tian. "Trends in World Military Expenditures, 2022." Stockholm International Peace Research Institute Fact Sheet. Stockholm: SIPRI (April 2023), https://doi.org/10.55163/PNVP2622.

2013. This is only the second time such plans have been announced. Some specialists say they are the most important defense documents to come out in postwar Japan.[65] The three policy documents are:

(1) "National Security Strategy"—it assesses the threats posed by China, North Korea, and Russia and the ways and means needed to meet the threats.

(2) "National Defense Strategy"—outlines a ten-year plan to improve the planning, execution and capabilities of the armed forces.

(3) "Defense Buildup Program"—outlines priorities and the step-by-step increases in defense spending.

In these documents, there are three noteworthy aspects of the security strategy. First, the introduction of long-range missiles with a span of one thousand miles, which will give Japan the capability of striking targets deep within an aggressor's territory. Presently, Japan only has short-range missiles to intercept incoming aircraft, missiles, and drones that penetrate Japan's air space. This is a fundamental shift from *senshu boei* (defense-oriented) policy that Japan has followed since the Occupation. Since Japan does not have long-range missiles in its inventory, it will have to purchase them from other countries. In the long run, the plan calls for Japan to produce its own long-range missiles.

Second, there is an allowance for Japan to develop and promote military alliances with a number of countries in the Indo-Pacific

---

65. Commentaries on the new security strategies can be found in the following sources: Sheila A. Smith, "How Japan is Doubling Down on Its Military Power." Council on Foreign Relations, December 20, 2022, *www.cfr.org* > article > how.japan.doubl…; Adam P. Liff and Jeffrey W. Hornung, "Japan's New Security Policies: A Long Road to Full Implementation." Rand Corporation, March 2i7, 2023, *www.rand.org* > … > Blog; Hideshi Tokuchi, "Japan's New National Security Strategy and Contribution to a Networked Regional Security Architecture." Center for Strategic and International Studies, June 23, 2023, *www.csis.org* > analysis > japans-new-nat…; Jingdong Yuan, "Japan's New Military Policies: Origins and Implications." Stockholm International Peace Research Institute, February 2, 2023, *https://www.sipri.org* > about > bios.

region. This is essentially a form of collective security, enabling Japan to project its military force beyond its borders. Starting with the US-Japan Security Treaty, the alliances have expanded to other treaty allies of the US, including South Korea, the Philippines, Thailand, Australia and New Zealand. China's hegemonic moves into the South China Sea, Southeast Asia, and certain Pacific islands brought India and Vietnam into the fold of the Indo-Pacific alliance. These agreements allow for dialogues among the leaders, joint military exercises, sharing of intelligence, and mutual access to each other's military bases.

Third, there is a substantial projected increase in military spending over five years. The annual defense budget will roughly increase two-thirds each year, and by 2027 is projected to total 8.9 trillion yen ($67 billion in 2023 rates). It will be close to 2 percent of GDP and is a massive amount of money, making Japan's defense budget the third largest in the world.[66] A high priority is given to the research and development of new weapons, so Japan can purchase their own manufactured military equipment. Meanwhile, Japan has to buy these sophisticated weapons from the United States. In January 2024, the Japan Ministry of Defense signed an agreement to purchase four hundred US tomahawk cruise missiles. With related equipment and services, the cost is $1.7 billion.[67]

The new security strategy is an ambitious and comprehensive project. It will require an enormous amount of funding to carry out and require a combination of sources. An increase in tax is one option, but will face strong opposition from Diet members, even from LDP members. Taxes are unpopular among the voters, so politically it is fraught with danger. Other sources could be debt spending, spending cuts, and moving resources from various budgets. Meeting budgetary goals is difficult because of contending domestic priorities—everybody wants their piece of the pie. But there is a glimmer of hope. Surprisingly, there is popular support for the security strategy plan. Due to the Chinese and North Korean threats, many Japanese are willing to see an increase in defense spending and an expansion of the SDF's capabilities.

---

66. Liff and Hornung, "Japan's," *www.rand.org* > ... > Blog.

67. Tomahawk cruise missiles can accurately deliver a thousand-pound warhead to a target more than one thousand miles way. Each missile costs about $2 million.

Therefore, significant developments domestically and internationally have led to major changes in the objectives of Japan's defense planning. Constitutional restraints are still obstacles to fulfilling the objectives of the strategic security plans. There is a need to revise or amend Article 9, but there are only three distinct possibilities: first, Article 9 could be abolished completely; second, there could be amendments and/ or revisions; and third, maintain the status quo. The first option is completely out because Article 9 has become a "sacred" provision of the constitution supported by the vast majority. The third option is unsatisfactory and is the reason why serious discussions have taken place for over seventy years. This leaves only the second option of some form of revision or amendment.

There are two basic challenges facing the LDP and its coalition partners. Presently, the ruling party and its partners have the necessary votes in the National Diet, a two-thirds majority of both chambers, but the first challenge is to persuade the Diet, specifically the members of the coalition, to come to an agreement within and between the parties to decide how to revise a part of the constitution. The LDP could decide on a single proposal approach, where all the energy and attention are on one item. It helps to prioritize what is most important and avoid distractions. An example would be the legitimizing of the SDF as an armed force. Former Prime Minister Abe suggested adding a simple sentence, "recognizing the legitimacy of the Self-Defense Forces." Another approach is to offer a set of revisions or amendments. This would widen the stakes and allow for trade-offs and a balancing of support. However, broadening the approach allows those who want a comprehensive change to enter with their ideological and emotional appeals. Pragmatic reasoning is overwhelmed, opposition develops, and it is difficult to bring everybody together to form a solid voting bloc. Obviously, both approaches have pitfalls. There is also the possibility of procedural change, moving to a simple majority vote. This is a big change, a slippery slope that could have severe consequences. Most legislators would not want to go this route; it would face fierce opposition.

The other challenge is to persuade the voters. Legislators, as politicians, are fully aware of what the majority of their constituents want, as their careers depend upon voters' support. One way to capture the voters' response to a particular issue is through public opinion polls. Public opinion is primarily measured in Japan by newspaper polls. The major newspapers are *Asahi Shimbun, Yomiuri Shimbun, Mainichi Shimbun,* and *Nikkei* or *Nihon Keizai Shimbun.* The news agencies, *Kyodo News* and *Jiji Press* conduct periodic polls. In addition, the government runs polls through the Cabinet Office, as does the public broadcasting system, NHK *(Nippon Hoso Kyokai)* Japan Broadcasting Corporation. There is some bias built into the newspaper polls. The *Asahi* is liberal, the *Yomiuri* is conservative, and the *Nikkei* is business oriented. The bias is due to what questions and how they are asked, but the differences are slight and do not distort the overall view of public opinion.

There are generational differences in public opinion. Three generations have passed since the present Japanese Constitution was proclaimed. For a long period in postwar Japan, public opinion was stable with few pronounced changes. The older generation that lived through the Hiroshima and Nagasaki atomic bombings and the bombing of almost all the major cities of Japan have a visceral reaction to any war. It is often said Japan suffers from a "nuclear allergy," an aversion to the use of nuclear power. This aversion is not a sickness to be cured. It is a fundamental, broad-based opposition towards nuclear weapons. The antinuclear movement first gained widespread support from the Bikini Incident. On March 1, 1954, a fallout from a US hydrogen bomb test on the Bikini Atoll in the Marshall Islands spread radiation over a vast area of the Pacific. A Japanese fishing vessel, which was outside the danger zone designated by the US became a victim of the radioactive ashes. Upon returning to Japan, twenty-three crew members were hospitalized with radiation sickness, and one later died. There was fear that fish caught in the Pacific were contaminated. Anxiety over public safety from nuclear radiation was aroused, and a protest letter demanding the banning of hydrogen bombs received millions of signatures. This was the beginning of the antinuclear organization.

A further concern about nuclear weapons arose when it was discovered that they were stored on American bases in Japan. The storage of nuclear arsenal was sizable in Okinawa. It started with the Korean War and grew in size during the Vietnam War. Nineteen different types of nuclear weapons and around 1,200 nuclear warheads were in storage. It was an open secret. The secret agreement between Japan and the US on nuclear weapons storage had no Japanese text because the Japanese officials wanted to avoid criticisms in case of a leak. In 1969, while the agreement was being updated in Washington, the document was leaked.[68] But the Okinawans were already suspicious of nuclear weapons stored at an ammunition depot, and their fear was proven correct when in 1968 a B-29 bomber aborted its takeoff and nearly crashed into the depot. The truth came out about the near nuclear disaster. It was 1972 when the nuclear weapons were finally withdrawn when Okinawa reverted back to Japanese control.

The Japanese government was sensitive about the nuclear issue. In 1959, Prime Minister Kishi instituted the "Three Non-Nuclear Principles"—no production, no possession, and no introduction of nuclear weapons. Japan would neither develop nuclear weapons nor permit them on its territory. But such an idealistic statement was not based on the realities of that time. The Japanese officials consented to the storing of these weapons because of security concerns in the midst of the dark days of the Cold War.

Nuclear-armed US warships were also regularly visiting Japanese waters and ports. These visits, plus the storage of nuclear weapons, especially on Okinawa, were constant irritants that strained US-Japan relations. They became part of the anti-American protest movements organized against the Mutual Security Treaty, the stationing of US troops in Japan, and the Vietnam War.

These events from the 1960s to the 1980s demonstrated how domestic and external factors had an impact on public opinion and voters. Incidents continued to occur, heightening antiwar feelings, and the degree of opposition was enough to prevent any changes in Article 9. The fear about nuclear power did not go away. The Fukushima Daiichi Nuclear Power Plant disaster of March 2011 rekindled the fear.

The antinuclear movement is part of a larger, more diverse movement called pacifism. Pacifism peaked in the early days of postwar Japan. For a population that had suffered the experience of war and was

---

68. Robert S. Norris, William M. Arkin, and William Burr, "Where They Were, How Much Did Japan Know?" *The Bulletin of the Atomic Scientists* 56, no. 1 (January-February 2000): 11-13, 78-79.

undergoing extreme deprivation, it is easy to see why they would be emotionally drawn to the ideals of peace. Article 9 came to represent and popularize pacifism, and it rapidly developed into a popular cult.[69] In the political arena, it had the support of several organizations, but its primary support came from the Japan Teachers' Union (*Nikkyoso*) with its peace education program and leftist groups within the Japan Socialist Party.

There are groups that support the pacifist phrases in Article 9 because they are viewed as vested rights and advantages for their own cause. These organizations feel any effort to revise or delete the pacifist clause needs to be vigorously opposed. Once Pandora's box is opened, and revision is made, it may lead to other drastic changes. Women and labor organizations are vigilant in the protection of their rights. Vested groups have become entrenched and are ready to push back on any threat to change pacifist phrases, for they view this as a threat to their areas of concern.

The antinuclear and broader pacifist movements have seen a decline for two reasons. First, they face a paradoxical situation, which is revealed in public opinion polls. A clear majority oppose Japan being involved in any conflict abroad, for example, Afghanistan and Iraq. But the same majority support rearmament for purposes of self-defense. In other words, it is legitimate to use force to defend one's soil but not to use force to help allies defend against threats to their soil. Would the allies come to your aid if you were attacked? The need for militarization has overtaken the ideal of demilitarization. Secondly, the younger generation is not sufficiently disturbed by the lack of transparency—an explanation of what path the government would take for self-defense—nor are they emotionally consumed with a sense of victimization. Furthermore, they are far removed from the horrors and fears of war. Living in an affluent society, not directly involved in a war, young people do not have the strong desires of the older generation to join in protest movements.

Recent polls have shown many Japanese remain ambivalent on certain constitutional issues. Overall, the public supports Japan's Constitution

---

69. Fukui, "Twenty Years," 54.

and opposes attempts at revision. In Article 9, the response is mixed. Slightly more voters are against changes in the article, with LDP members strongly supporting changes, but other coalition members are evenly split in their support. When it comes to the SDF, a majority support its role in disaster relief and humanitarian and rehabilitation missions but are opposed to its use abroad in policing and controlling violence. Today, because of international developments, the majority want the SDF to be constitutionally recognized and those favoring the expansion of its size and capabilities have increased, but they are slightly in the minority. Therefore, over 50 percent of voters support the current interpretation of self-defense, but they have reservations about the extended role of the SDF abroad.

The significance of public opinion is undeniable. It influences whether there are to be any changes in Article 9, and how it is interpreted and implemented. The role of the SDF, its capabilities and functions are all influenced by public opinion. Paul Midford, an American political scientist who teaches at Meiji Gakuin University in Tokyo, concludes, "Japanese public opinion is influential because it is stable, coherent, and, regarding attitudes about the utility of military force, not easily or quickly swayed by elite attempts to influence it. Japanese public opinion matters because it has a significant influence on Japanese foreign and security policies."[70]

The prospect for a constitutional revision or amendment seems brighter today than ever before. The LDP and coalition partners have more than the necessary two-thirds of votes in both chambers, but this is only on paper and not guaranteed. The public support for the SDF has been increasing. The government's plan to almost double the defense spending within five years and to provide the SDF with counterstrike capabilities has been increasing but still does not have sufficiently broad support. Voters have mixed feelings, and with a two-thirds vote necessary in a national referendum, it is a high hurdle. Though the prospects are better, it is still going to be a tedious process. The failure of conservative governments to move ahead on constitutional reforms is the result of their inability to bring together party factions

---

70. Paul Midford, *Rethinking Japanese Public Opinion and Security: From Pacifism to Realism?* (Stanford: Stanford University Press, 2011).

and coalition partners. In addition, the lack of broad popular support has delayed or blocked all efforts at reform.

Revision is inevitable, but it will probably be in small incremental steps. So far, rearmament has proceeded rather smoothly with support from the conservative party and the business community, which profits from the procurement contracts. The operation of the SDF will essentially be the same. New weapons and technology will be introduced and constantly upgraded. Offensive capabilities will be enhanced, which poses a question—can a country's intentions be inferred from the offensive capabilities it develops? Strategic thinkers can evaluate a nation's capabilities but can only make a guess at its intentions, and on this basis make a judgment. So, it remains a crucial question.

There have been no innovations in regard to Article 9. The words have remained the same, and the only changes have been in the interpretation and reinterpretation of the words. What has been proposed is the changing of the words or the adding of a phrase or two. It would not significantly change the size, role, functions and capabilities of the SDF. Instead, it would provide symbolic value to the revision and legitimize the SDF and its actions. The revision would proclaim Japan as an independent, main actor in global security issues. National pride would be enhanced, and other nations would have a different view of Japan as one of the major powers in the world.

PART II
TERRITORIAL DISPUTES

SETTLEMENTS AND CONTROVERSIES

CHAPTER FOUR

Japan is an island nation comprised of four main islands surrounded by 6,852 islands and islets 0.1 km or more in circumference. If every piece of rock jutting from the sea is counted, there are about fourteen thousand. Japan is somewhat similar to the United Kingdom, except the UK is surrounded by far fewer islands. Compared to a landlocked country or a country that is adjacent to another country, the boundary of an island nation is clearly defined and established; in fact, the boundary is permanent. In contrast, the boundary of a landlocked country is often the result of a war or a large-scale political upheaval such as a revolution or forced annexation. The victor gains territory, while the loser relinquishes some of its territory. Moreover, a treaty arrangement can change the boundary. The boundary is not permanent.

For land-based nations, the boundaries tend to follow geographical features such as large rivers and mountain ranges, and there are exceptions where boundary lines cut across rivers, mountains, and other geographical features. Boundaries even divide racial and language groups, defining and separating them. A notorious example of boundary-making was the practice by colonial powers in Africa, who drew boundaries in a straight line for simplicity's sake. Unfortunately, tribes and language groups were separated by such practices. Today, countries in Africa have to live with boundaries drawn by the colonial powers.

One would think the island nations would have no problems with their boundaries. If an island can be seen with the naked eye, there is no doubt who has jurisdiction over the island. But what about those islands many miles away? How far does a nation's sovereignty extend? In the early 1800s, European countries came to an understanding that a country's sovereignty extends three miles from the "baseline," which is essentially the coastline, the line that forms the boundary between the land and the sea. Three miles was arbitrarily chosen because it was the maximum range of coastal cannon of that time. Soon, with the advancement of technology, the three-mile standard became obsolete. Seafaring countries led the movement to change the distance to twelve nautical miles (nm). The twelve nautical miles limit is known as the "territorial waters" or "territorial sea," and it was standardized in 1982 by the United Nations Convention on the Law of the Sea (UNCLOS).[71]

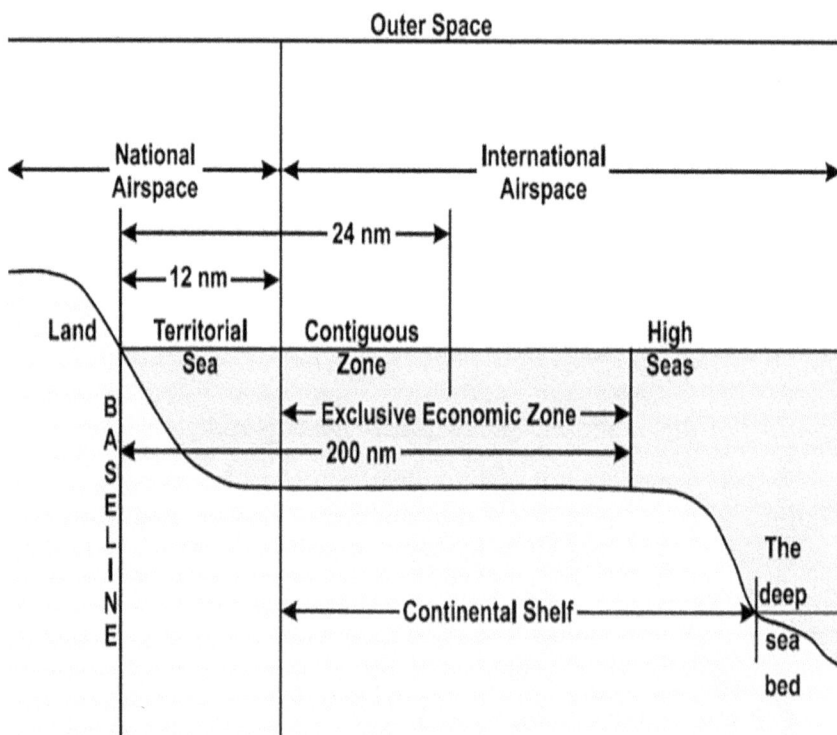

UNCLOS zones

---

71. At its ratification in 1982, 117 states signed. Presently, over 165 states plus nonmembers such as the European Union have signed. The United States has not signed the convention and does not recognize UNCLOS as a customary codification of international law. Nevertheless, it is considered to apply to states regardless of whether or not they have signed the convention.

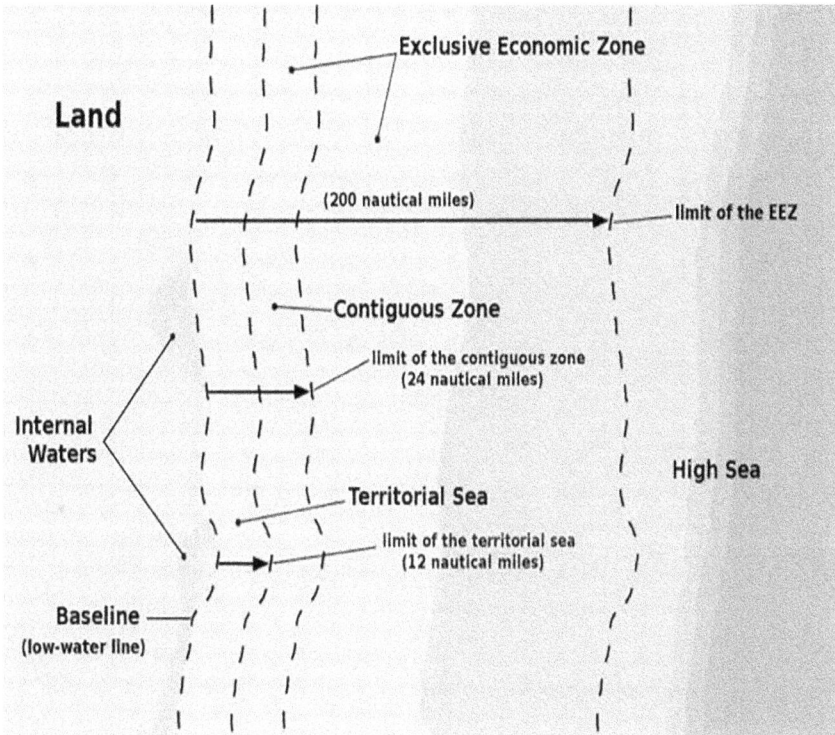

Aerial view of zones

All measurement of distance begins from the baseline, but it is not a simple matter. The UNCLOS lists three different types of baselines:

1. normal baseline — low-water line drawn along the coast.

2. straight baseline — when the coast is deeply indented, has fringing islands, river mouths, and bays, line is drawn outside the projections.

3. archipelagic baseline — joining the outermost points of the outermost islands and reefs.

Therefore, distances may vary depending on what type of baseline is being used. The strength of one's claim is dependent on the certainty of the baseline.

When the sovereignty over the territorial waters is extended, the airspace above, the seabed below, and the subsoil are all included in the claim. The distance over water is measured in nautical miles. It is based on the earth's longitude and latitude coordinates, with one nautical mile equaling one minute of latitude. A nautical mile is slightly longer than a mile; one nm is equal to 1.15 land-measured (statute) mile. For sea navigation, the nautical mile is easier to calculate than the statute mile.

The quest for extending a nation's sovereignty is unending. Coastal nations began to claim a "contiguous zone." As defined in the UNCLOS, it is the area of the ocean adjacent to the territorial sea and extending another twelve nm beyond the territorial sea, making it a maximum of twenty-four nm from the baseline. In this area, the coastal state has the authority to enforce regulations pertaining to customs, fiscal, immigration or sanitary laws.[72] But it does not have total control. The "right of innocent passage" allows a foreign vessel to transit through another country's territorial waters or contiguous zone, as long as the ship does not engage in any actions that are a serious or unacceptable threat to the coastal state. This right of innocent passage is a principle of customary international law and is part of the UNCLOS. Although UNCLOS protects freedom of navigation for military ships, there is controversy over what constitutes a serious or unacceptable threat. Can it be used for surveillance purposes?

The biggest change came with the introduction of the "exclusive economic zone" (EEZ). As prescribed in the convention, it is the area beyond and adjacent to the territorial sea, extending out from the territorial sea to a maximum distance of two hundred miles from the baseline. The coastal state is given sovereign rights to the marine resources on the surface and below the surface, including the seabed and subsoil.[73] The exclusive rights include the air space above. Furthermore, under Article 60 of the UNCLOS, artificial islands, installations and structures can be built in the EEZ. Since an EEZ can be drawn around each island claimed by a country, the overall EEZ can be extensive. Japan has a vast EEZ because of its many islands.

---

72. *https://www.un.org* > unclos > part2.

73. *https://www.un.org* > unclos > part5.

Another part of the ocean addressed in the convention is the continental shelf. The continental shelf comprises the seabed and subsoil of the undersea areas that extend beyond the territorial sea throughout the natural prolongation of its land territory to the outer edge of the continental margin, or a distance of two hundred nautical miles from the baseline. Due to the slope and shape of the continental shelf, they vary from nation to nation. In those cases where natural prolongation allows, the maximum distance from the baseline could be extended to 350 nm. All of this area belongs inherently to the coastal state.[74] In the case of the EEZ, the coastal state with the continental shelf controls its resources on the surface and below the surface of the sea. Japan vehemently objected to the provision of the 1958 Convention on the Continental Shelf, which gave coastal states sovereign rights over living organisms on the continental shelf. The Japanese government did not sign the convention because it would limit Japanese fishermen from catching fish and crabs from several areas around the globe.

Another boundary-setting zone that is not part of the Law of the Sea but often works in conjunction with it is the Air Defense Identification Zone (ADIZ). This is the airspace of a country plus an additional wider area over land and water in which the identification, location, and control of all aircraft is required for national security purposes. They differ from country to country and have to be declared unilaterally. ADIZ is not proscribed in any international treaty and is not recognized by an international organization. It was first initiated by the US in 1950 at the height of the Korean War. About twenty countries have ADIZ, including the US, Japan, South Korea, North Korea, China, Taiwan, and Russia.

In the case of Japan, its ADIZ covers most of its exclusive economic zones. It was created by the US armed forces during the Korean War. It is extensive. For example, Japan's sovereignty covers the entire Ryukyu archipelago, and when the ADIZ was extended from the southernmost island, it overlapped that of Taiwan. The use of ADIZ by nation-states has caused serious problems of overlap, creating friction between countries.

---

74. *https://www.un.org* > unclos > part6.

While the UNCLOS helps to define maritime boundaries by its definition of various zones, it does not cover how claims can be made for uninhabited islands. To make these claims, nations have depended on customary international law. During the Age of Discovery, roughly from the fifteenth century to the seventeenth century, European explorers discovered uninhabited islands, which were referred to as *terra nullius* (Latin for "land belonging to no one"). Since they discovered the islands, they claimed these islands for their respective countries. All that was required was to land on the island and plant the national flag. In some cases, aborigines were living on the islands, but these natives did not count, and the Europeans viewed the islands as unoccupied. This principle of claiming ownership of supposedly uninhabited islands is known as the Doctrine of Discovery. It was an excuse for colonial conquest, asserting the superiority of European people with their culture and religion. From the eighteenth century onward, the Doctrine of Discovery was increasingly found to be insufficient in establishing a claim. By the mid-twentieth century, countries began to demand actual occupation for a legitimate claim to be made, and international courts began to support this view. There had to be physical evidence of housing and other facilities to show this was, as the courts emphasized, an "effective occupation." Fishermen making periodic visits to an island did not constitute a valid claim to ownership of the island.

Although the UNCLOS does not address how a claim is made for an island, the ownership and control of the natural resources both in the ocean and in the seabed and subsoil is clearly stated—they belong to the coastal state. This is of utmost importance. There is an abundance of sea life in the waters of the EEZ and along the continental shelf. Fishing is a major industry in Japan and a primary food source. The waters around the islands are rich fishing grounds.

There are other rich resources available on the ocean floor. In the 1960s, findings began to be published, citing the rich mineral deposits on the seafloor. Governments began to take notice in the 1970s and made claims to the ocean's mineral resources. Oil and gas deposits are now known to exist near several of the islands being contested between Japan and its neighbors. Vast quantities of polymetallic nodules, also known as manganese nodules, can be found on the surface of the seabed of the EEZ and continental shelf. They contain manganese, silicates, and iron oxides. On the ocean floor are massive sulphide deposits. Valuable minerals found on the ocean floor and in the crusts attached to rocks include cobalt, nickel, iron, copper, silver, zinc, and rare earth minerals. Manganese is important in the manufacturing of steel by providing strength. Minerals, such as cobalt, nickel and manganese are crucial ingredients in green energy products. They are key components in the manufacturing of batteries used in electric vehicles, solar cells, wind turbines, and many tools and gadgets. These minerals are essential elements in the production of computers, cellphones, and other electronic devices.

The International Seabed Authority of the United Nations, which oversees the regulation of deep-sea mining, is preparing to accept mining permit applications. This is the beginning stage of deep-sea mining. Technology exists for large pumps to vacuum materials from the seabed, while robots and specialized machines with artificial intelligence pluck nodules from the seafloor. The whole process is complex and will take a few years before operations can begin. The effect on the environment is unknown, so environmental impact studies need to be completed before deep-sea mining can commence.

WARTIME PLANNING

In comparison to the planning for the status of the emperor and the imperial institution, and the restrictions placed on the future rise and use of militarism, the question of the small islands surrounding Japan was seldom considered. This is understandable because these islands were of no strategic use at that time and had little economic value. However, the small islands needed to be mentioned within the broader question of what to do with the territories acquired by Japan through conquest or colonization.

During the early phase of World War II, the question of territorial disputes and settlements was handled by the Subcommittee on Territorial Problems, which was under the Advisory Committee on Postwar Foreign Policy. It covered problem areas like the Japanese

Mandated Islands, Okinawa, Kurils, and Southern Sakhalin.[75] The Mandated Islands or South Seas Mandate were islands awarded to Japan by the League of Nations in the aftermath of World War I. They were part of the German Empire. The subcommittee left the Mandated Islands for the postwar planners to settle. After the war, the Allies decided to designate the islands as the UN Trust Territory of the Pacific Islands. Today, they have been separated into the Palau, the Northern Mariana Islands, the Federated States of Micronesia, and the Marshall Islands.

On Okinawa, the subcommittee was divided. A minority advocated a tougher approach, stripping Japan of everything. They felt the committee was too lenient towards Japan. Indeed, the majority did take a generous, liberal view. Most of them were willing to have Japan retain control of small and adjacent islands, which became known as the "minor islands." Although Okinawa is not that small, being the fifth-largest island of Japan, in their view, it is part of the Ryukyu archipelago and is considered an "adjacent" island and belongs to Japan.

On the opposite side of Japan, on the north, lies the Kuril Islands, an archipelago of eighteen islands, not counting islets. It extends northeast from the Japanese island of Hokkaido to the southern tip of the Kamchatka Peninsula, which is part of Russia. Directly north of Hokkaido is Sakhalin, a large, elongated island that belongs to Russia. Japan had no interest in Sakhalin until the nineteenth century, and even then, it was of peripheral interest. Japanese fishermen were the first to settle in Sakhalin. Russians arrived in 1853 and moved into the northern part. Both countries agreed to share control of the island, but in 1875, Russia acquired all of Sakhalin in exchange for the Japanese controlling the Kurils.

As a result of the Russo-Japanese War of 1904-05, Japan gained possession of the southern half of Sakhalin at the 50th parallel and gave it the Japanese name of Karafuto; it became a Japanese colony. This gain was affirmed in the Treaty of Portsmouth brokered by President Theodore Roosevelt, and it formally ended the war.

---

75. Borton, *Spanning*, 93.

The Cairo Declaration of 1943, issued by the wartime allies of the United States, United Kingdom, and Republic of China (ROC or Taiwan), stated that Japan "will be expelled from all territories which she has taken by violence and greed." The principle of stripping Japan of all the colonies acquired from war was developed by the Subcommittee on Territorial Problems. This committee worked alongside the Far East Area Committee of the State Department on the drafting of the declaration in August of 1942. South Sakhalin or Karafuto was returned to Russia in 1945 because it was a colony of Japan and was acquired through a war. Today, Sakhalin with the Kuril Islands forms the Sakhalin Oblast (province) of Russia.

The handling of Sakhalin was clear-cut, but not so with the Kuril Islands. During wartime planning, most American planners considered the Kurils part of Japan, especially the four islands closest to Japan. It was not a colony and was not acquired in a war. Instead, it was given to Russia, and the reason for this will be explained in the following section on wartime conferences. Japan has a strong claim to the four southernmost islands of the Kurils because of its proximity to Hokkaido and the long history of settlement by a large number of fishermen. This historical background is covered in chapter 5.

WARTIME CONFERENCES

There were three wartime conferences held by the Allied powers that touched on territorial questions. The first was the Cairo Conference held on November 23, 1943, and attended by President Franklin D. Roosevelt, Prime Minister Winston Churchill, and Generalissimo Jiang Jieshi (aka Chiang Kai-shek). From this conference emerged the Cairo Declaration, proclaimed on December 1, 1943, which laid down principles governing postwar territorial settlements. The declaration read in part:

The Three Great Allies are fighting this war to restrain and punish the aggression of Japan. They covet no gain for themselves and have no thought of territorial expansion. It is their purpose that Japan shall be stripped of all the islands in the Pacific which she has seized or occupied since the beginning of the First World War in 1914, and that all the territories Japan has stolen from the Chinese, such as Manchuria, Formosa and the Pescadores shall be restored to the Republic of China. Japan will also be expelled from all other territories which she has taken by violence and greed. The aforesaid three great powers, mindful of the enslavement of the people of Korea, are determined that in due course Korea shall become free and independent.[76]

A couple of issues in the declaration pertaining to small island sovereignty should be noted. First, China was allowed to regain a vast amount of territory. Jiang Jieshi even wanted control over the Ryukyus to return to China, but the declaration did not make any reference to the future jurisdiction of these islands. Roosevelt supported Jiang Jieshi so China would keep fighting Japan. American officials assumed the Republic of China had the potential to be a great power, was sufficiently unified, and able to control and effectively administer these territories. The assumption proved to be wrong, and it did not take the Chinese Communists long to take complete control over all of China. Most historians agree the Cairo Declaration intended to give Jiang greater prestige and prop up his regime, but it did not succeed, and this misstep had enormous consequences for East Asian politics.[77]

Another troubling issue was the clause, "Japan will also be expelled from all other territories which she has taken by violence and greed." The word "territories" was not broken down. Such broad language left much to interpretation, and officials assumed whatever they wanted. Is the Kurils one of these "territories?" Several American planners during the war did not consider the Kuril Islands a territory to be returned because it was assumed to be a part of Japan. Unfortunately, it was not stated as such in the document. Because of the ambiguity of

---

76. Department of State. *Treaties and Other International Agreements of the United States of America, 1776-1949* (Washington, DC: Government Printing Office, 1969), 858.

77. Herbert Feis, *Churchill, Roosevelt, Stalin: The War They Waged and the Peace They Sought* (Princeton, NJ: Princeton University Press, 1957), 532. Charles M. Dobbs, *The Unwanted Symbol: American Foreign Policy, the Cold War, and Korea, 1945-1950* (Kent, OH: Kent State University Press, 1981), 12.

the terminology, small islands could be added or deleted under the rubric of "territories," but even large islands could be a problem. For example, was Okinawa one of those territories "taken by violence and greed?" Before the Cairo Conference in July 1943, the Subcommittee on Territorial Problems drafted a document proposing policies toward Okinawa that were independent of those toward Japan. It recommended the detachment of Okinawa and the rest of the Ryukyus from Japan and suggested three alternative solutions: (1) transfer the Ryukyus to China, (2) place them under international administration, or (3) let them be conditionally retained by Japan. The planners had a long-term fear that if Okinawa was returned to Japan, it would need to be under international surveillance to prevent Japan from militarily using the island as a stepping-stone for future expansion.[78] As it turned out, the US planners preferred the second option cited above, and the administrator was to be the United States. According to Masahide Ota, a noted historian and former Okinawa governor, the detachment, or separation from Japan proper of Okinawa, was largely determined at the time of the drafting of the Cairo Declaration. It was not unusual for American planners to have such a view. Even some Japanese officials in those days, before the signing of the San Francisco Peace Treaty in 1951, did not consider Okinawa to be an integral part of Japan.[79] By detaching Okinawa from Japan proper, Okinawa could be included in the territories "taken by violence and greed." Hence, Okinawa would not be under the sovereignty of Japan but would be under US administration. Sovereignty would be administered directly by the US military, whereas in Japan Proper, SCAP, and not the US military, would govern indirectly using the Japanese government. In the context of that time, this interpretation was important. Under military rule, Okinawa could serve as a defensive bulwark against the rising tide of communism in Asia. Considering the long period of Japanese control over Okinawa, Japan's sovereign rights to Okinawa were justified, but strategic concerns preempted historical and legal arguments. Japan had to wait until 1972, when the Vietnam War ended before it could regain its sovereign rights to Okinawa. This is an excellent example of how a

---

78. Masahide Ota, "The U.S. Occupation of Okinawa and Postwar Reforms in Japan Proper," in Ward and Sakamoto, *Democratizing Japan*, 296-97.

79. Ota, "US Occupation," 301.

major power, the United States, took advantage of the ambiguous text of a wartime declaration and through interpretation, gained control of a territory for strategic purposes.

Regarding the first option of transferring Ryukyus to China, there is no record of such an offer in the files of the State Department. It may have been discussed, but no official offer was made. Nevertheless, it is said that President Roosevelt informally offered Okinawa to Jiang, but Jiang did not follow up on the offer.[80] The purported incident of the offer of Okinawa illustrates the potential problem that could arise between planning and implementation. Personal action on the part of Roosevelt infuriated some policy planners. Roosevelt had his own preconceived ideas, preferring Korea under a trusteeship of the US, China plus two other powers, and the mandated islands be internationalized. Obviously, he was not an expert on East Asia, and Japan was not one of his top priorities. Dr. Stanley K. Hornbeck, chairman of the Far East Area Committee, hinted that Roosevelt made personal decisions on important postwar policies without consulting Secretary of State Cordell Hull or the rest of the Department of State. Roosevelt had the propensity to ignore or pay little attention to the State Department. It was no secret that there was a wide rift between the White House and the State Department. The president showed his choice of advisors by taking only military advisors to Cairo, except for one or two State Department interpreters.[81] Even the experts on Japan in the State Department were ignored, and Roosevelt did not consult with them before the Cairo Conference. Dr. Borton said he and Dr. Blakeslee did not participate in the drafting of the declaration and only learned about it when the communique was released.[82]

One problem the Cairo Conference left in limbo, as alluded to in the last sentence in the declaration, was the question of Korea. When will Korea attain its sovereignty? If not immediately, what temporary arrangement will be made? The question engendered a wide range of

---

80. Ota, 297.

81. Borton, *Spanning*, 98-99.

82. Bruce Cummings, *The Origins of the Korean War, Vol. 1: Liberation and the Emergence of Separate Regimes, 1945-1947* (Princeton, NJ: Princeton University Press, 1981), 40, 107.

responses. One group believed Korea should remain a Japanese colony. Another group thought it should be controlled by China, Russia, or an international body. Then there were those who believed it should be independent. This last group formed the majority and was spearheaded by Borton and Blakeslee.[83] The United Kingdom delegation inserted the phrase, "in due course," giving vagueness to the timing. But the Americans inserted the word "independent," thus assuring Korea would be free and independent from foreign control.

The next conference where territorial issues were discussed was the Yalta Conference of February 4-11, 1945. In attendance were President Roosevelt, Prime Minister Churchill, and Premier Joseph Stalin. The Axis powers were in full retreat in Europe and the Pacific. The major objective of the conference was to discuss the surrender and occupation of Germany and the postwar reorganization and security of Europe. Although of secondary importance, it was necessary to discuss Allied policy in the war against Japan, particularly the plan for Soviet intervention in the Pacific War. In addition, plans had to be made for the dismantling of the Japanese empire.

In preparation for the conference, Hugh Borton and George Blakeslee prepared major papers, with Borton doing one on Korea, while Blakeslee did one on the Kuril Islands. The Blakeslee paper on the Kurils was more critical because the Russians demanded the islands as part of the conditions for entering the war with Japan. Dr. Blakeslee argued Russia had a substantial claim to the northern group of islands but little justification for its claim to the southern islands. The islands closest to Hokkaido, he stressed, were an integral part of the territory of Japan. He recommended southern Kuril be retained by Japan, and that central and northern islands be placed under an international trusteeship.[84] Blakeslee's recommendations were not followed. President Roosevelt used the Kuril Islands as an incentive for the Russians to engage in the Pacific War. Roosevelt gave possession of the entire Kurils to Stalin in exchange for his promise to enter the war within ninety days after the surrender of Germany. Churchill was excluded from this conversation. Roosevelt went to Yalta determined

---

83. Borton, *Spanning*, 80.

84. Borton, 123.

to have the Soviets involved in the Pacific War, for he believed without Soviet intervention, the war with Japan would be a drawn-out fight with huge casualties.

In the Yalta Declaration, what constitutes the Kuril Islands is not explained, but this omission is critical. Eighteen islands in this archipelago have claimed ownership partly based on proximity to the mother country. Japan claims only the southernmost four islands, known in Japan as the "Northern Territories." To this day, Russia has cited the Yalta Agreement to support its argument that the Northern Territories are part of the Kurils and under its sovereignty. Japan's position is that the four islands are not part of the Kuril Islands. Blakeslee tried to clarify the issue in his paper, but his analysis was not accepted. According to Borton, President Roosevelt sidestepped the State Department and was poorly prepared for the meetings with Churchill and Stalin. The briefing books, which included Blakeslee's report and SWNCC papers, were never used by Roosevelt.[85] They were simply ignored.

The third and final wartime conference discussing territorial problems was the Potsdam Conference, which was held southwest of Berlin from July 17 to August 2, 1945. President Roosevelt had died, the war in Europe was over, and Japan was on the brink of defeat. The allied leaders were President Harry Truman, the successive United Kingdom prime ministers Winston Churchill and Clement Attlee, and Premier Joseph Stalin.

On July 26, 1945, the conference issued the Potsdam Declaration, which detailed the terms for the unconditional surrender of Japan. The key passage in the declaration is Article 8, which reads as follows, "The terms of the Cairo Declaration shall be carried out and Japanese sovereignty shall be limited to the islands of Honshu, Hokkaido, Kyushu, Shikoku and such minor islands as we determine."[86] This statement introduced more ambiguity regarding Japan's territorial sovereignty. Questions immediately arose about the meaning of "minor islands" and who controls these islands. Although Dokdo, Senkaku, and other

---

85. Borton, 126.

86. Department of State. *A Decade of American Policy: 1941-1949, Basic Documents* (Washington, DC: Historical Office, Department of State, 1950), 28-40.

"minor islands" were discussed in planning sessions and negotiations, they were not mentioned in any of the wartime documents. Why did the Potsdam Declaration and other documents fail to define what is meant by "minor islands" and not specifically mention Dokdo and Senkaku? The declaration was initially based on a paper prepared by Blakeslee and Borton a full year before the conference. Later on, there was some input by British officials and by those in the War Department. The government officials and Japan specialists assumed the "minor islands" remained under Japanese sovereignty. This underlying liberal view was widely held by American officials and carried into the San Francisco Peace Treaty conference. Since these assumptions about Japan's rights to the "minor islands" were never put into writing, there was no validation of the planners' thinking and, therefore, no way to legitimize their positions. In the absence of any written statements, Japan was allowed to exercise de facto sovereignty over these ill-defined islands. As time went on, the territorial issues continued to be left ambiguous, and when Cold War factors intervened, vagueness was politically and strategically preferred.[87] Even among the Allies, there was a lack of political and legal consensus as to how the territorial rights to these islands were to be settled. John Foster Dulles, the chief negotiator of the peace treaty grew impatient and said that while the Allies quarreled about what to do, the conference simply had to move on, and to leave for the future the resolution of these problems by using "international solvents" rather than the treaty. By "international solvents," Dulles meant the International Court of Justice or diplomatic negotiations.[88]

While the Potsdam Declaration did not clarify the island issues, SCAP decided to step in and began to define territories under Japan's sovereignty. It issued SCAPIN-677 which defined the four main islands of Japan (Hokkaido, Honshu, Kyushu, and Shikoku) and approximately one thousand smaller adjacent islands to be under the control of Japan. A few notable islands such as Tsushima and the Ryukyu Islands, were listed to be under Japanese sovereignty, but Takeshima, Habomai,

---

87. In contrast to the Cairo Declaration, where Okinawa was not included as an integral part of Japan, the Potsdam Declaration included Okinawa as a "minor island" under Japanese sovereignty. Strategic Cold War considerations were the reasons for the change.

88. Foreign Ministry of Japan, Treaties Bureau, *Heiwa joyaku no teiketsu ni kansuru choso*, 7:267-84.

Shikotan, and some other small islands were specifically excluded from Japanese political and administrative control. Takeshima is a group of islets between Korea and Japan, while Habomai and Shikotan are part of the Kurils. However, paragraph 6 clearly states, "Nothing in this directive shall be construed as an indication of allied policy relating to the ultimate determination of the minor islands referred to in Article 8 of the Potsdam Declaration."[89] Sovereignty over a minor island like Takeshima was to be determined at a later date.

Six months later, on June 22, 1946, SCAP issued SCAPIN-1033, which defined the areas where Japanese were permitted to engage in fishing and whaling. The boundary line was known as the "MacArthur Line."[90] Dokdo was outside the MacArthur Line; therefore, Japanese fishing boats were not permitted to operate near Dokdo and were prohibited from approaching within 12 nm of Dokdo. SCAPIN-677 and SCAP-1033, with its MacArthur Line, seem to provide South Korea with the opportunity to claim Dokdo. The South Korean government moved to claim Dokdo on grounds that SCAP excluded Japanese control of Dokdo. But Japan rebutted this claim by pointing to paragraph 6 of SCAPIN-677. SCAPIN-1033 had a similar disclaimer in paragraph 5, stating, "The present authorization is not an expression of Allied policy relative to the ultimate determination of national jurisdiction, international boundaries or fishing rights in the area concerned or in any other area." Such ambiguity led to counterclaims which made resolving the dispute all the more difficult.

As the negotiation and drafting of the San Francisco Peace Treaty reached its final stages, the South Korean government learned Dokdo was not in the peace treaty, and the MacArthur Line would be abolished with the signing of the treaty.Korea demanded Dokdo be included in Article 2 (a) listing islands reverting to Korea from Japan, and the MacArthur Line be maintained. The request was denied by Assistant Secretary of State Dean Rusk. In his letter to the Republic of Korea government, dated August 10, 1951, he stated: "Dokdo was

---

89. SCAPIN (SCAP Instructions or Index) is a directive. SCAPIN-677 can be accessed through *https://www.mofa.go.jp* > pdfs.

90. SCAP-1033 is available in the Ministry of Foreign Affairs of Japan's website: *https://www.mofa.go.jp* > takeshima.

never treated as part of Korea and, since about 1905, has been under the jurisdiction of the Oki Islands Branch Office of Shimane Prefecture of Japan. The island does not appear ever before to have been claimed by Korea."[91]

With no hope of a change in the peace treaty, the South Korean government decided to take action before the signing and the abolishment of the MacArthur Line. South Korean President Syngman Rhee announced the "Syngman Rhee Line" on January 18, 1952, three months before the peace treaty became effective. It ran along the continental shelf about 200 nm offshore. Dokdo was now clearly placed under South Korean sovereignty.

SAN FRANCISCO PEACE TREATY

The San Francisco Peace Treaty, signed on September 8, 1951, officially ended the state of war between Japan and the Allied Powers and allowed Japan to regain full sovereignty. It ended the Allied Occupation of Japan. Forty-eight nations were signatories, but the absence of two countries was significant. China was not invited due to disagreements on who should represent the Chinese people—the Republic of China (ROC) or the People's Republic of China (PRC). Korea was not invited because of a similar disagreement on who should represent the Korean people—South Korea or North Korea. The Soviet Union was a participant but did not sign the treaty. It opposed the treaty for several reasons, but its major objection was that it was designed by the US to draw Japan into a military coalition against the Soviet Union.

The nonsignatory Soviet Union and the absentee China and Korea each viewed the development and the final signing of the peace treaty with regret if not anger. Already, the Soviets had occupied the Kurils, which they argued had been given to them lawfully, even if not explicitly stated in the peace treaty. The Soviets claimed the entire Kurils was undeniably their territory. China and Korea felt they were left out of the treaty and not part of Japan's postwar settlement. They wanted every

---

91. Department of State. *Foreign Relations of the United States, 1951* (Washington, DC: Government Printing Office), 6:1206.

bit of territory they were entitled to even though the island sovereignty issues were not clearly defined. This was the beginning of rumblings over the disputed islands.

The turmoil over the omission of the contested islands was not due to the incompetence of the peace treaty drafters or because they were oblivious to the issues. The islands were purposely omitted for strategic reasons. During the drafting of the treaty, the Cold War had intensified, and the erstwhile partners became virulent foes. The US and the Soviet Union were vying for dominance in East Asia. As a result, views of the US changed drastically, thus impacting each small island dispute. Due to competing claims, the Kurils and Dokdo, in particular, became contentious issues. The US policymakers supported Japan's sovereign rights to the islands as a defense against communist aggression in East Asia, but they had difficulty deciding whether to mention or omit the islands in the treaty. The American planners finally decided to postpone the resolutions. There was now an opportunity to separate some of the islands from the Kurils and place them under Japanese control, which would have pleased Japan, a potentially valuable ally in the struggle against the communist bloc in East Asia. Such a decision would have angered the Soviets, who were already complaining bitterly about the draft peace treaty and would have made it extremely difficult to work with them on other vital issues. Similarly, a decision on Dokdo could have been made at the time of the peace treaty negotiations, but it proved to be too difficult with the start of the Korean War. The focus then was on working with the allies rather than taking on a divisive issue. Therefore, the small island questions were omitted from the peace treaty, and an opportunity to settle these territorial disputes was missed.[92]

The following excerpts, pertaining to territorial sovereignty, are from Article 2 and Article 3 of the peace treaty:

---

92. Minoru Yanagihashi, "The Territorial Questions in East Asia and San Francisco Peace Treaty: Historical Perspective." Paper presented at the Association for Asian Studies 2011 Annual Conference, Honolulu, April 2011, 10-11.

Article 2

(a) Japan, recognizing the independence of Korea, renounces all right, title and claim to Korea, including the islands of Quelpart (Chejudo), Port Hamilton (Komundo) and Dagelet (Ulleungdo).

(b) Japan renounces all right, title and claim to Formosa and the Pescadores.

(c) Japan renounces all right, title and claim to the Kurile Islands, and to that portion of Sakhalin and the islands adjacent to it over which Japan acquired sovereignty as a consequence of the Treaty of Portsmouth of September 5, 1905.

Article 3

Japan will concur in any proposal of the United States to the United Nations to place under its trusteeship system, with the United States as the sole administering authority, Nansei Shoto south of 29 degree north latitude (including the Ryukyu Islands and the Daito Islands)…Pending the making of such a proposal and affirmative action thereon, the United States will have the right to exercise all and any powers of administration, legislation and jurisdiction over the territory and inhabitants of these islands, including their territorial waters.[93]

The Cold War induced changes in the drafting process. How did these changes take place? In the case of Dokdo, the drafting procedure is fully documented, and it is interesting to follow the process. Initial planning for the peace treaty began in early 1947, and a first draft of the treaty was prepared by the Bureau of the Far Eastern Affairs of the State Department. The chairman of the drafting committee was Hugh Borton. The drafting of the peace treaty was a tedious process with

93. United Nations Treaty Collection, "Treaty of Peace with Japan. Signed at San Francisco, on 8 September 1951." *Treaty Series* 48, 50, 1952, https://treaties.un.org > unts. In Article 2 cited above, the Korean names for the islands are given in parentheses and do not appear in the text of the treaty. Nansei Shoto in Article 3 is the Japanese name for the Ryukyu Islands. Daito Islands and Okinawa are part of the Ryukyu chain of islands.

no fewer than eighteen drafts. As drafts of the peace treaty were being prepared, territories were added or deleted. In the beginning drafts, Dokdo was included among the islands given to Korea in Article 2 (a). Then the drafts began to show Dodo as a territory of Japan. In the last series and the final draft, Dokdo was completely omitted. Cold War calculations were taken into account, as American drafters were worried about a possible Communist takeover of the Korean peninsula. There was even the suggestion that Quelpart (Chejudo in Korean), which is clearly a part of Korea, could be taken over by Japan to stem the Communist tide. Dokdo would then serve as a military buffer under the control of the Japanese. Obviously, security worries about the Korean War and the Cold War directly impacted the thinking of the drafters.

The turmoil in East Asia and the intensification of the Cold War not only affected the text of the peace treaty but also the timing of the conference. There were two contending approaches. One approach was taken by the Joint Chiefs of Staff and the Defense Department. They wanted to delay the peace preparation because of worsening relations with the Soviet Union. The defense officials wanted continued and complete access to bases in Japan, a right that might be affected by a treaty. The other approach was to have the policymakers move as rapidly as possible in the negotiation and drafting of the treaty. John Foster Dulles, who tirelessly negotiated the treaty and was a staunch anticommunist, pushed for a quick treaty. Others urging an early signing of the treaty included General MacArthur, the State Department, and Asian specialists. It made sense to these leaders and planners to quickly help Japan regain its sovereignty, help the economy recover, and democratize the country. It would make Japan a useful and valuable partner in East Asia. Japan was reevaluated as a possible ally in the anticommunist strategy. Cold War pressures allowed the fast approach to win out. However, the fast approach did little to solve the territorial sovereignty disputes. In fact, it made negotiations much more difficult with the constraint on time.[94]

---

94. Yanagihashi, *"Territorial,"* 11. Borton made a special trip to Tokyo to discuss with MacArthur the draft of the peace treaty. Both agreed it should be signed as soon as possible.

Since the Soviet Union, South Korea, and China were not signatories to the San Francisco Peace Treaty, separate peace treaties had to be negotiated with the three countries. The Soviet-Japanese Joint Declaration concluded on October 19, 1956, ended the state of war and restored diplomatic relations between the countries. It was a declaration that normalized relations between the countries, but it was not a peace treaty largely because of the territorial dispute. The Russians agreed to hand over the Habomai Islands and Shikotan to end the dispute, but Japan would not get the other two islands, Kunashiri and Etorofu. Initially, the Japanese accepted the offer, but the US objected to this deal and threatened to keep the Ryukyu Islands if Japan gave away the other two islands. The importance of this threat has been a point of debate among historians. As a result, Japan rejected the offer, and the negotiation fell apart. No peace treaty has yet been signed, and the Kuril Islands dispute continues.

Japan's relationship with South Korea and China had similar results. After the San Francisco Peace Treaty concluded, it took over fourteen years, a total of seven sessions, before the Treaty on Basic Relations between Japan and South Korea was signed on June 22, 1965. It established diplomatic relations between Japan and South Korea, settled property problems and claims, and promoted economic cooperation. However, it failed to resolve the Dokdo dispute, and the issue was set aside so the treaty could be signed. It took longer to reach a peace treaty with China. The Treaty of Peace and Friendship between Japan and the People's Republic of China concluded on August 12, 1978. Negotiations on the treaty began in 1974, hence it took four years. The Senkaku issue was a stumbling block, so it was set aside to resolve at a later date.

In retrospect, the San Francisco Peace Treaty was the progenitor of the small island sovereignty disputes. The Northern Territories of the Kurils and Dokdo are not mentioned in the text of the treaty, but in prior negotiations, these issues were vehemently discussed. Therefore, the territorial disputes could be traced back to the time of the treaty. On the same day that Japan regained its sovereignty with the signing of the peace treaty, it signed a mutual security treaty with the US. The treaty allowed for American bases and the stationing of military personnel, thus making Japan a close ally and supporter of US Cold War policies.

This alignment of Japan with the US is known as the "San Francisco System."[95] It is the most notable legacy of the peace treaty. With the ending of the Occupation, the US maintained administrative control over Okinawa and did not relinquish it until 1971, when Okinawa and the Senkaku Islands were transferred to Japan. Soon after, China contested Japan's claim over the Senkakus. Today, we live with the legacies of the peace treaty.

---

95. John W. Dower, "The San Francisco System: Past, Present, Future in U.S.-Japan-China Relations," *The Asia-Pacific Journal* 12, issue 8, no. 2 (February 23, 2014).

SMALL ISLANDS DISPUTES

—————————— CHAPTER FIVE ——————————

Why all this fuss about small islands? At first glance, they seem to be puny and insignificant. They appear peaceful and idyllic but have taken on a different image.

The islands being disputed are similar in many ways. They are the results of volcanic actions, massive rock formations erupting out of the oceans. The islands have few broad, flat areas. Sheer rocks cliffs, plunging into the ocean make for a fascinating sight; they would qualify for a picturesque postcard. But they are not so welcoming. Dokdo and Senkaku Islands are difficult to reach, especially Dokdo, where landing is possible only when the weather permits and the ocean is calm, which is extremely rare.

There are some differences. The Kuril Islands (Northwest Territories) are cold and wet most of the year, whereas the Senkaku Islands have tropical and semi-tropical climates. The Kuril Islands and Dokdo are inhabited, albeit by a few people, while the Senkaku Islands are uninhabited.Although inhabited, both the Kurils and Dokdo are unpleasant places. Despite the low temperatures, high humidity and constant fog, the Kurils are populated by small communities engaged in sulfur mining, hunting and fishing. Dokdo has a small garrison, but it serves no purpose other than occupying space. To subsist on the islands is a formidable logistical problem as food and drinking water are not available. The Kurils are close together and their rich fishing grounds provide a food source. Dokdo is not noted for its fishing, and the fishing ground of the Senkakus has not been fully exploited. Both islands are seen more as potential sources of valuable seabed minerals. In terms of location, they are all strategically located. Dokdo in the Sea of Japan and Senkaku in the East China Sea are in busy shipping lanes, while the Nemuro Strait between Hokkaido and the Kurils is limited to local transit.[96]

The islands are known by different names. Dokdo has three names—Dokdo in Korean, Takeshima in Japanese, and Liancourt Rocks in English. Dokdo in Korean means "Solitary Island," Takeshima in Japanese means "Bamboo Island," while Liancourt Rocks has a historical meaning. It is named after the French whaling ship Le Liancourt, which nearly crashed on the rocks in 1849. The four islands in contention in the Kuril Islands are grouped together and called the "Northern Territories" by Japan, but each island has Russian and Japanese names. The Japanese government uses "Northern Territories" to emphasize its position that the four islands are not part of the Kurils and are an "inherent" part of Japan—they are in the "northern" part of Japan Proper. The last group of disputed islands is Senkaku, which is the Japanese name, and Diaoyutai in Chinese. The name used is critical because it provides evidence that the country has possession of the territory. If a Chinese map shows the islands as "Senkaku Islands," it is admitting the islands are under Japanese sovereignty. Therefore, the name of the islands on a map or document is of utmost importance. Throughout this book, I have chosen the names most frequently used in literature and by the mass media. They are as follows:

A.   Kuril Islands/Northern Territories—Habomai Islands (consisting of ten islets), Shikotan, Kunashiri, and Etorofu

B.   Dokdo/Takeshima

C.   Senkaku/Diaoyutai

When the narrative is from the perspective of a particular country, and the documents cited are from that nation, I have used the name employed by that nation.

---

96. For background information on the three islands, see: Ocean Policy Research Institute (OPRI), *Review of Island Studies*. The research papers are part of the program of the Sasakawa Peace Foundation, a private foundation and think tank. https://www.spf.org/islandstudies.

KURIL/NORTHERN TERRITORIES

The Kuril Islands are in an archipelago, consisting of fifty-six islands and many islets. It stretches from the Russian Kamchatka Peninsula to the northeast coast of the Nemuro Peninsula of Hokkaido. Japan's claim to the Kuril Islands has been narrowed to the four southernmost islands, Habomai Islands, Shikotan, Kunashiri and Etorofu. The four islands are known as the "Northern Territories" in Japanese, but the Russians call them the "Southern Kuril Islands." Habomai consists of ten islets plus various rocks, but they are combined and referred to as "Habomai Islands" or simply as "Habomai." Habomai and Shikotan are much smaller and represent only 7 percent of the disputed territory. They are close to Hokkaido; Habomai is less than five miles from Hokkaido. Japan declared the Northern Territories are part of the Nemuro Subprefecture of Hokkaido Prefecture and, therefore, are not part of the Kuril Islands.

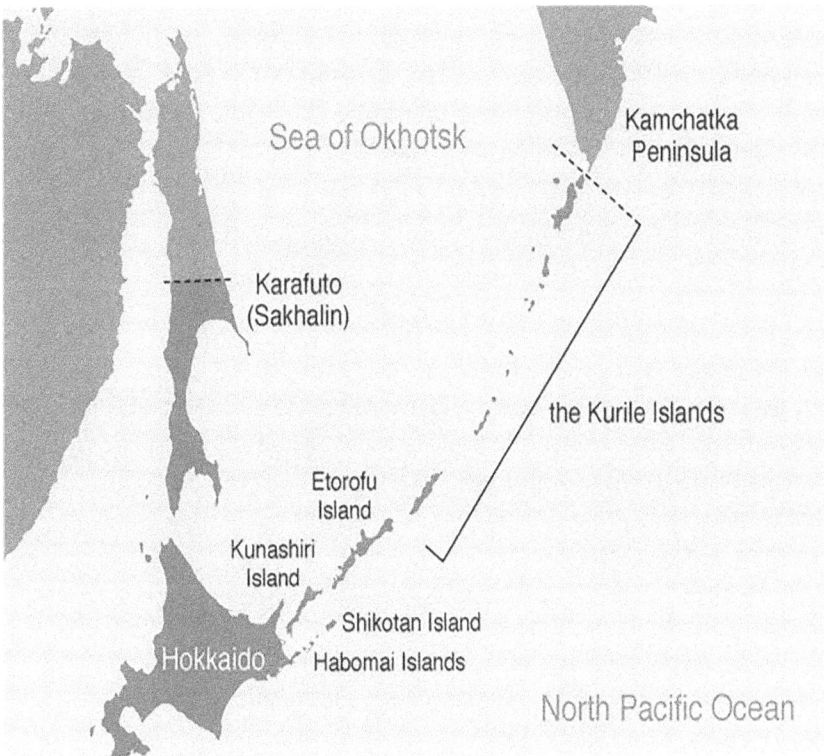

Kuril Islands and Northern Territories

Habomai Islands

Japanese fishermen have been plodding the waters of the Kurils for many years, and by the mid-nineteen century, some of them had settled on these islands. Interest in the northernmost part of Japan picked up in the eighteenth century. The area was long known as Ezochi, the land of the aborigine Ainu. Then, during the Tokugawa period (1600-1868), it became Yezo province. The name "Hokkaido" was first applied in the Meiji era (1868-1912).

Japanese writers began to point out the importance of Yezo and the surrounding territories in the eighteenth century. Foremost among the advocates for the economic development and colonization of Yezo, and by extension the neighboring islands, was Toshiaki Honda, a political economist and theorist.

In "A Secret Plan of Government," written in 1798, Honda warned about the increasing menace of the Russians and Japan's need to encourage colonization and prepare national defenses. On colonization, Honda wrote:

> If the islands near Japan were colonized, they would make highly desirable places. By such colonization numerous possessions—some sixty or more—would be created, which would serve not only as military outposts for Japan, but would also produce in abundance metals, grain, and fruit, as well as various other products, thus greatly adding to Japan's

strength.... This is a matter of especial regret because there have been Russian officials in the islands inhabited by the Ainu since about 1765. They have displayed such diligence in their colonization efforts that eighteen or nineteen Kurile islands and the great land of Kamchatka have already been occupied. Forts are said to have been built at various places and a central administration established, the staff of which is regularly changed, and which rules the natives with benevolence. I have heard that the natives trust them as they would their own parents.

When the Ezo islands are colonized they will make worthwhile places which will yield several times as much produce as Japan does today. Although there are other islands both to the east and west which should also be Japanese possessions, I shall not discuss them for the moment. At this crucial time when the Ezo islands are being seized by Russia, we are faced with an emergency within an emergency. When, as now, Japan does not have any system for colonizing her island possessions, there is no way of telling whether they will be seized by foreign countries or remain safe. This is not the moment for neglect; such actions by foreign powers may lead to the destruction of our national defense.[97]

Russia began to explore and send missions in the 1770s. By the mid-1800s, Russian settlements had reached a point where increasing quarrels with the Japanese necessitated the need to have an arrangement to settle disputes. On February 7, 1855, the Treaty of Shimoda was signed, creating the boundary between Japan and Russia with a line between the islands of Etorofu and Uruppu. Japan had ownership of Etorofu and all the islands extending southward, while Russia had control over Uruppu and all the islands north of it. Sakhalin was left open and to be under joint sovereignty. Twenty years later, on May 7, 1875, Japan and Russia signed a new treaty wherein Japan relinquished all rights to Sakhalin in exchange for Russia giving up all rights to

---

97. Donald Keene, *The Japanese Discovery of Europe: Honda Toshiaki and Other Discoverers,* 1720-1798 (London: Routledge and Kegan Paul, 1952), 170-72, 178.

the Kuril Islands. The next change occurred when Japan emerged victorious in the Russo-Japanese War of 1904-05. In the Treaty of Portsmouth, Japan gained possession of the southern half of Sakhalin at the 50th parallel. The southern tip of Sakhalin is about fifty miles from Hokkaido. When the Soviet Union declared war on Japan in August 1945, one of its main objectives was to gain possession of Southern Sakhalin and the Kuril Islands. Immediately, Soviet troops invaded and occupied Southern Sakhalin and the Kurils and have been there ever since. All Japanese inhabitants, approximately seventeen thousand, were expelled by 1947. There is evidence the Soviets had intended to occupy Hokkaido after the Japanese surrender in August 1945. At that time, the US was willing to have the Russian troops participate in the Occupation, but only if they were under the command of General MacArthur. The Soviets refused to have their troops under SCAP. Japan was fortunate that the Soviets did not participate in occupation policies.[98]

Russia continues to cite the sentence in the Yalta Agreement: "The Kuril Islands shall be handed over to the Soviet Union." They believe the explicit language justifies their claim. However, Japan and the US argue the Yalta Agreement and the San Francisco Peace Treaty do not delineate what constitutes the Kuril Islands. Japan claims the Northern Territories are not part of the Kuril Islands relinquished in the peace treaty but are "inherent" territories of Japan. The United States agrees with the Japanese position.[99] The US maintains the Cairo Declaration does not explicitly mention the Kuril Islands as one of the territories Japan will be expelled from, and the Potsdam Declaration does not clarify what is meant by "such minor islands as we determine," so this phrase could be used to justify the transfer of the Northern Territories to Japan. Japan has argued the long history of settlement has made these islands "inherent" territories, and the influence of the Japanese is

---

98. Martin E. Weinstein, *Japan's Postwar Defense Policy, 1947-1968* (New York: Columbia University Press, 1971), 29.

99. For the Japanese position, see Kiyoaki Tsuji, ed., *Shiryo—sengo nijunenshi* (Tokyo: Nihon hyoronsha, 1966), 1: 661. For the US position, see Bruce A. Elleman, Michael R. Nichols, and Matthew J. Ouimet, "A Historical Reevaluation of America's Role in the Kuril Islands Dispute," *Pacific Affairs*, 71, no. 4 (Winter 1998-1999): 489-504.

seen even today. Recent visitors have confirmed this and commented on how the islands seem to be more Japanese than Russian.

The Russian position is there are no "inherent" territories. Boundaries are political, artificial, and fixed by conquest or international agreements. According to their point of view, these islands of the Kurils have become Russian territory through a series of international agreements, and this de facto control is permanent.

During the 1956 peace negotiation between Japan and the Soviet Union, the Soviets offered to return Habomai and Shikotan, reluctantly admitting the islands were Japanese. After initially accepting the offer, the Japanese circled back to the "four island return," making it clear that all four islands constitute the Northern Territories and cannot be separated. The Soviet Union withdrew its offer.[100]

Ever since the 1956 Joint Declaration, there has been no substantial change in the positions taken by the two sides. Feeble attempts were made at the highest level of government, but nothing of substance has emerged. Some concessions have been made by the Russians, such as visa-free trips for those Japanese wishing to visit ancestors' graves and for Japanese fishermen to fish in Russia's EEZ.

The waters around the Kurils are rich fishing grounds, allowing for cooperative projects. There are mineral deposits, including sulphur, iron, copper, and gold, but they have not been explored and mined to any degree.

The fisheries agreements of 1984, 1985, and 1998 were concluded to alleviate the somewhat strained relationship between Japan and Russia. Further negotiations have been stymied by the nonexistence of a maritime boundary between the two countries. The controversy over the Northern Territories has made it extremely difficult to negotiate boundary lines extending from the Sea of Japan to the Sea of Okhotsk and out to the Pacific Ocean.[101]

---

100. Richard deVillafranca, "Japan and the Northern Territories Dispute: Past, Present, Future," *Asian Survey*, 33, no. 6 (June 1993): 610-24. For more information on Japan's attempt to seek international support for its position, see Kimie Hara, *Japanese-Soviet/Russian Relations Since 1945: A Difficult Peace* (New York: Routledge, 1998).

101. Seokwoo Lee, ed., *Encyclopedia of Ocean Law and Policy in Asia-Pacific* (Boston: Brill/Nijhoff, 2023), 110.

Tension flared up when Russian President Dmitry Medvedev visited Kunashiri Island on November 1, 2010, the first time a Russian leader had visited the Kurils. Japanese Prime Minister Naoto Kan protested, and Russia retorted, saying Medvedev was planning a return trip. This was a highly visible and symbolic move, and the Japanese government considered it a serious provocation. It led to the deployment of advanced missile defensive systems in the Kuril Islands the following year. Periodically, Russia has upgraded its missile systems and additionally deployed amphibious assault ships and other vessels to its Pacific Fleet.

Prime Minister Abe made several attempts to rekindle the talks on the disputed islands. He visited Moscow in April 2013 and spoke with President Vladimir Putin and again met with Putin in Vladivostok in September 2018 and in Moscow in January 2019. None of these meetings produced a breakthrough. The parties were far apart on the issue of the islands and attempts to improve relations with Russia through economic development, joint tourism projects, and diplomatic talks failed to persuade the Russians to return the islands.

Instead, Russia has increased its military presence in the Northern Territories. Beginning in 2015, satellite imagery and media reports showed Russian airstrips, barracks, antiaircraft missile bases, and other infrastructure have been constructed. The facilities built on Kunashiri Island are as close as ten miles from Hokkaido. In the last five years, the construction of bases in the Kuril chain has significantly increased. Besides surface-to-air missile systems, anti-ship missile battalions were deployed on Etorofu and Kunashiri, the two largest islands of the Northern Territories. These missiles have the range to strike most ships sailing around Hokkaido. The substantial increase in personnel, along with the supporting infrastructure, suggests these are permanent deployments.[102]

Strategically, the Kuril Islands are more important for Russia than for Japan. The island chain separates the Sea of Okhotsk from the Pacific Ocean and is a transit point for Russia's Pacific Fleet stationed at Vladivostok to enter the Pacific Ocean. In addition, the islands serve as forward bases for defensive purposes and intelligence gathering.

---

102. Ike Barrash, "Russia's Militarization of the Kuril Islands." Center for Strategic and International Studies (September 27, 2022), *https://www.csis.org* > blogs > russia...

Japan applied sanctions on Russia shortly after the invasion of Ukraine in February 2022, ending all economic cooperation with the Russians around the Northern Territories. Russia retaliated by halting peace talks over the Kuril and ending a fisheries agreement with the Japanese. In September 2022, Russia revoked the agreement, allowing former Japanese residents of the islands visa-free visits. At about the same time, Russia and the PRC conducted a naval exercise, the Vostok 2022.[103]

These rising tensions make it all the more important to maintain consultations with Russia. Through diplomatic, economic, or other means, strenuous efforts are required to damper further militarization and avoid the accidental use of force.

DOKDO/TAKESHIMA

Dokdo is a couple of islets in the Sea of Japan between South Korea and Japan. It is 215 km to Korea and 220 km to Japan; almost equidistant from both countries.[104] Another measurement used is the distance to the closest occupied island. Dokdo is 92 km to South Korea's occupied island of Ulleungdo (Dagelet in French) and 160 km to Japan's occupied Oki Islands. The closeness of Dokdo to a South Korean-populated island is often used to bolster South Korea's claim to the islets.

---

103. Ike Barrash, September 27, 2022.

104. 1.609 kilometers (km) equal one mile (mi). Therefore, a mile is longer than a kilometer.

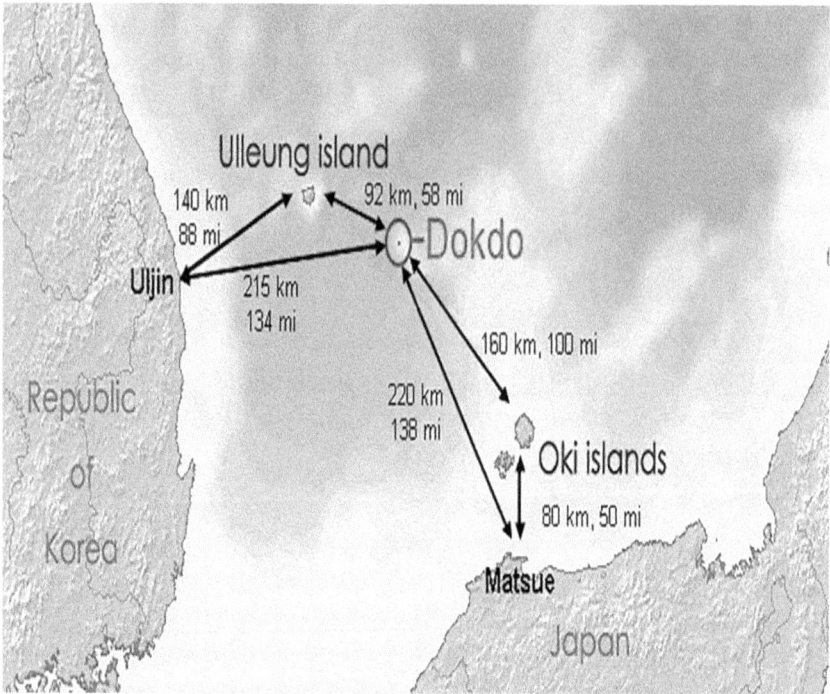

Dokdo with distances

Dokdo islets

Rocky formations with little clear space make it difficult to land on the islets. It is only possible to disembark if a landing pier has been built. At certain times of the year, Dokdo is inhospitable because of the cold wind. The sea around the islands becomes rough, making landing impossible. Some weeds grow, but the bare rocks cannot sustain trees. Food has to be brought in, and drinking water transported. There is water, but it is contaminated with dung from the birds. In need of exploration is the seabed, which is said to be rich in gas as well as minerals.

In the early years of the twentieth century, sea lion hunting was popular around Dokdo. The competition became fierce and was hurting the sea lion hunting business. Yozaburo Nakai, a resident of the Oki Islands, who had a sea lion hunting business, petitioned to have the islands incorporated into a Japanese territory to stabilize the hunting business. The cabinet of the national government decided to take up the issue, and shortly thereafter claimed sovereignty over the islands.[105]

On February 22, 1905, the Governor of Shimane Prefecture issued a proclamation that the islands, now officially named "Takeshima," were under the jurisdiction of the Oki Islands branch of the Shimane Prefectural Government. The Japanese government used the principle of *terra nullius* to justify its claim of sovereignty. Before 1905, Japanese fishermen visited the islands but were never inhabitants. With the incorporation of Takeshima into Shima Prefecture and the recognition of Nakai's sea lion hunting business, Japan could use the argument of "effective occupation" to support its claim of sovereignty as required by customary international law.

The Japanese Ministry of Foreign Affairs states, "Takeshima is indisputably an inherent territory of Japan, in light of historical facts and based on international law." Referring to early documents and maps and the activities of Japanese fishermen in the area, Japan claims it had established sovereignty over Takeshima by the middle of the seventeenth century. Up to this point, no other country had settled or claimed Takeshima. The cabinet decision of 1905 reaffirmed Japan's sovereign rights over Takeshima.[106]

---

105. *https://www.mofa.go.kr* > contents.

106. Ministry of Foreign Affairs of Japan. *https://www.mofa.go.jp* > asia-paci. The name Takeshima is used in this section because this is how the islets are referred in Japanese and US documents.

Japan refers to the San Francisco Peace Treaty as confirmation that Takeshima is Japanese territory. In the drafting process of the treaty, the US rejected South Korea's attempt to include Takeshima as one of the territories to be renounced by Japan. As evidence of the unstated position of the US government, Japan points to one sentence in Dean Rusk's letter: "Dokdo (Takeshima) was never treated as part of Korea…" By intentionally excluding Takeshima, the treaty confirmed Japan's sovereignty over Takeshima. With these arguments in hand, Japan claims the present occupation of Takeshima by a South Korean garrison is illegal.

The use of historical records to substantiate claims for remote uninhabited islands is common, and in the case of Dokdo, the Korean historical documents are more substantial than those of the Japanese. South Korea's claim to Dokdo is based on a number of classical Korean texts, of which the *Chronicles of the Three Kingdoms* is probably the most important. It was recorded in 512 that Dokdo and Ulleungdo were discovered by the Silla Kingdom. Discovery by itself was not enough, so documents were produced showing the actual Korean occupation of the islands. These documents proved Ulleungdo to be inhabited, and in most cases, Dokdo was figuratively mentioned with Ulleungdo.[107]

In the early seventeenth century, Japanese were allowed by their government to travel to Ulleungdo to hunt for sea lions, gather abalone and other marine resources, and establish fisheries. These activities came into conflict with those of the Koreans. Tokugawa shogunate, the Japanese government of that time, decided to withdraw since no Japanese had settled in Ulleungdo, and the island was closer to Korea. An agreement was reached in 1696 with Korea. At the same time, the shogunate decided to ban travel to Ulleungdo. According to the documents held by South Korea, the shogunate had ceded sovereign rights over the islands to Korea. Japan claimed there was a mix-up in communication, and their documents show the shogunate did not cede the sovereignty over the islands.

There were other incidents concerning fishing and smuggling, and each time government edicts were issued maintaining Korean

---

107. See Pilkyu Kim, *Claims to Territory Between Japan and Korea in International Law* (Bloomington, IN: Xlibris, 2014). Documents and maps are extensively examined.

sovereignty over the islands. The islands were not always occupied. During the period of Manchu domination, Koreans withdrew from the islands, but contacts and visits were maintained. In 1881, a recolonization policy brought back Korean settlers and helped to justify Korea's rights of sovereignty based on effective territorial occupation.

Japan did not protest these actions by Koreans. At that time, the documents and even the official maps showing Dokdo under Korean rule were not challenged. All this changed in 1905 when Japan annexed Korea as a colony after years of political coercion, intimidation, and fighting. Colonization lasted for forty years.

South Korea regained its sovereignty in 1945 with the end of World War II but did not regain ownership of one of its islands, Dokdo, which was laid aside during the peace treaty negotiations. However, South Korea bluntly exerted its sovereign rights with the Syngman Rhee Line on January 18, 1952. It extended South Korea's boundary beyond 200 nm along the continental shelf. Dokdo was included in the large territorial zone created by this act. The line was eventually abolished in 1965 with the signing of a Japanese-South Korean fishing agreement.

The involvement of SCAP in creating boundaries and its role in sovereignty issues was previously discussed. Two SCAP documents, SCAPIN-677 and SCAPIN-1033, seemed to take away Japan's sovereignty rights over Takeshima. But in both cases, another part of the document included the disclaimer that the directive was not the final word and left the issue open. To this day, South Korea uses the SCAP directives to support its claim of sovereignty over Takeshima, while Japan denies such a claim could be made. The back-and-forth arguments continue.

During the Allied Occupation of Japan, US armed forces used Dokdo as a bombing range and notified Japan but did not announce its intention to South Korea. Ignoring of South Korea's involvement with Dokdo resulted in a tragedy. A bombing exercise in 1948 killed several Korean fishermen who were not informed.

Dokdo was placed unilaterally under South Korea's ownership and rule in 1954 when it was occupied by a detachment of South Korean volunteer guards. International law requires not only the stationing of personnel but also signs of permanent residency, like infrastructures. Over a period of time, the Koreans built a lighthouse, a storage facility, housing units, a promenade, and a docking jetty. Today, there are about thirty-seven security personnel, who serve on a rotational basis. As one can imagine, it is not a pleasant tour of duty. There is nothing to do, except some maintenance work, exercise, and playing games. Most volunteer for patriotic reasons, but it is a mental strain.

As expected, the Japanese and South Korean governments differ in their political and legal views about Dokdo, but the difference in popular support for Dokdo is quite remarkable. The South Korean government promotes nationalistic fervor by placing posters about Dokdo along streets and in trains. The response of the South Koreans has been much more emotional and nationalistic, marked by patriotic zeal. Whenever an incident occurs over Dokdo, there are protest marches, dancing, singing, chanting, beating of drums, and speeches. Sometimes extreme measures are taken. A mother and son protested by cutting off their fingers and a man self-immolated.

Another example of how South Koreans is consumed with Dokdo is the heavy demand to visit the islets. The South Korean government has included Dokdo in its promotion of tourism, but it has restricted the number of tourists due to limited facilities. South Koreans go to Dokdo as a pilgrimage, carrying small Korean flags; they play music, take endless selfies, and stroll along the promenade. The trip is viewed as a civic duty. A French photographer, who was taking photos of the islands, relates a tourist's response, "As a Korean, we always wanted to come here once in our lives. It means a lot that we finally made it."[108]

---

108. Alexandra Genova, "Two Nations Disputed These Small Islands for 300 Years." *National Geographic* (November 14, 2018). *https://www.nationalgeographic.com > ...*

Tourists visiting Dokdo

Despite the antagonism that developed between the Republic of Korea (ROK or South Korea) and Japan, there were a few negotiated settlements regarding access to surface and subsurface resources. Agreements were reached by temporarily skirting the controversial question of territorial sovereignty. In 1974, Japan and the ROK came to an agreement on the joint development of oil and gas resources, and in 1998, both countries entered into a fisheries agreement. Further negotiations have been blocked by the disputed sovereignty over Dokdo. Because of the sovereignty question, no definitive maritime boundary could be drawn for the EEZ and continental shelf in that part of the Sea of Japan, and as a consequence, there was no way to pinpoint where to explore and drill.[109]

It has been difficult to come to a reasonable solution regarding the sovereignty of Dokdo because of nationalistic fervor. Japan proposed in September 1954 that the dispute over Dokdo be referred to the International Court of Justice (ICJ). It made the proposal again in 1962. The ROK rejected the proposal both times. In addition, the US had also suggested the dispute be referred to the ICJ. Fifty years later, in August 2012, Japan proposed for the third time that the dispute over the sovereignty of Dokdo be referred to the ICJ, but once again it was rejected. Both countries have to consent for the ICJ to have effective

109. Seokwoo Lee, ed., *Encyclopedia*, 107-09.

jurisdiction over the dispute. The US wants both countries to settle the issue, but the ROK will only do this if the US supports its position. Ever since the San Francisco Peace Treaty, the US has learned to be careful not to take sides. It does not want to antagonize either ally, for it has mutual security treaties with both countries.

Why has the ROK refused? The ROK believes it already has sovereignty over Dokdo, so there is no need to go to the ICJ. To do so would be to admit it does not have sovereignty or is unsure about it. The ROK Foreign Ministry responded, "Dokdo is clearly part of Korean territory historically, geographically and under international law, and no territorial dispute exists. The Japanese government's proposal to take the Dokdo issue before the ICJ is not worth attention." As contemptuous as the reasoning given, it is similar to the argument by Japan in its treatment of the Senkaku dispute with China.[110]

The ICJ has successfully handled several sovereignty disputes over minor islands. Nation-states have resolved their differences through a rules-based approach, adhering to international law. Unfortunately, in the Dokdo dispute, nationalistic sentiments have overridden legal reasoning and even political considerations. Feelings of victimization are aroused, and bitter memories are recalled in this rising tide of patriotism. Four decades of brutal Japanese colonization cannot be forgotten and are constantly linked with the island dispute. In this atmosphere, it is extremely difficult to find a resolution through the rule of law.

SENKAKU/DIAOYUTAI

The Senkaku Islands (in Japanese) or Diaoyutai (in Chinese) are five small uninhabited islands, which include three islets charitably described as "rocks or reefs." The larger islands are mostly volcanic, and the smaller islands are mostly coral. These islands in the East China Sea are 90 nm (170 km) from Ishigaki Island, the second southernmost island in the Ryukyu archipelago; they are 90 nm (170 km) from Taiwan; 180 nm (330 km) from China; and 225 nm (410 km) from

---

110. J. Berkshire Miller, "The ICJ and the Dokdo/Takeshima Dispute," *The Diplomat*, May 13, 2014. *https://thediplomat.com* > authors.

Okinawa. The southernmost island of the Ryukyu chain is Yonaguni, which is only 150 km from the Senkaku Islands, so it is closer and would be a logical choice to serve as a reference point. However, it is smaller in size and population than Ishigaki; therefore, Japan prefers to use Ishigaki as a measuring point.

Senkaku Islands with distances

Senkaku Islands

The Japanese government became aware of the Senkaku Islands in the 1880s, and in 1895, the islands were incorporated into Okinawa Prefecture through a cabinet decision. Japan used the principle of *terra nullius,* wherein islands discovered to be unoccupied and not under the control of any country could be claimed. It was the same approach used in claiming Takeshima.

After the islands were incorporated and became Japanese territory, they were leased to Japanese entrepreneurs, who started a factory processing dried bonito and a business collecting feathers on Uotsuri Island, the largest island in the Senkakus. There were also business operations on Kuba Island. These businesses lasted until the 1930s. At one time, as many as two hundred people inhabited the two islands. But the population dwindled, and by the postwar period, the islands were uninhabited and remain so today.

The Senkaku Islands were ignored for a long period. They were not mentioned in the wartime conferences or the San Francisco Peace Treaty. However, the treaty placed Okinawa under US administration, and since the islands were part of Okinawa, they came under US control. US armed forces were already using the islands as a bombing range. In June 1971, the Okinawa Reversion Agreement between the US and Japan was signed, and Okinawa, including the Senkaku Islands, were returned to Japan. The Senkakus were again under the control of Japan.

At about the same time, in 1971, China and Taiwan officially asserted their sovereign rights over the Senkaku Islands for the first time. Chinese sovereignty claims relied weakly on historical records. During the Ming (1368-1644) and Quing (1644-1912) dynasties, Chinese envoy missions went through the Senkakus on their way to the Ryukyu Islands, but they never stopped and settled the islands. China supports its claims by referring to the records of the Ming and Quing, where the islands are listed with Chinese names. Furthermore, published Chinese maps showed the islands with their Chinese names. Japan did not object to the Chinese naming of the islands, but it did argue that the names and geographical closeness of the islands were insufficient conditions for asserting territorial sovereignty.

Back in 1895, when Japan claimed the Senkakus, China did not contest Japan's sovereignty over the islands. It was not until 1971, some seventy-five years later, that China began to cite the dynastic records and maps to counter the Japanese claim. What caused the Chinese government to suddenly take notice of the Senkaku Islands? In 1969, the UN Economic Commission for Asia and the Far East conducted a survey on coastal mineral resources and reported the discovery of large deposits of oil and hydrocarbons in the waters surrounding the Senkakus. Within two years, China was aggressively rejecting Japan's claim to the islands, contending the islands had been under Chinese sovereignty since ancient times. The Chinese explained the lack of response earlier was due to an absence of diplomatic relations between Beijing and Tokyo until 1972. But this excuse was superfluous because China was already lodging protests against Japan on other issues before 1972.Surely, they could have claimed the Senkakus earlier on the international stage, if they had a legitimate claim. The arguments and counterarguments began.

Arguments over territorial zones and infringements on territorial waters became increasingly prevalent. In the 1990s, Chinese fishing vessels were routinely entering and challenging Japan's territorial waters around the Senkaku Islands. A Japanese nationalist group decided to deter these intrusions by erecting two lighthouses. To further control the encroachments, the Japanese government sold the islands to a Japanese family in 2002 to help prevent private landings by Japanese and foreigners. It stopped privately owned Chinese fishing vessels, but a few years later, other types of Chinese ships entered the waters near the Senkakus. In December 2008, two ships of the State Oceanic

Administration of China entered the territorial waters around the Senkaku Islands. This became a government-promoted infringement.

Then, in September 2010, an ugly incident occurred. Two Japanese Coast Guard patrol boats were deliberately rammed by a Chinese fishing trawler. The incident turned into one of the biggest crises in postwar Sino-Japanese relations. For the first time, the Japanese government decided to take action and arrested the captain of the trawler. China responded by suspending diplomatic talks, cutting off export of rare earth metals used in the manufacturing of electronic devices and batteries, and seized four Japanese businessmen. Diplomatic tension grew until the captain was released. The Senkaku issue did not go away. The nationalistic governor of Tokyo, Shintaro Ishihara, threatened to have the city purchase the islands from the private owners because the government was inapt in protecting its sovereignty. To avoid angering Beijing and to diffuse the issue, the cabinet of Prime Minister Yoshihiko Noda decided to purchase the Senkaku Islands to nationalize the islands. The Chinese reaction to the purchase was immediate and heated. Anti-Japan demonstrations erupted in various parts of China, with Japanese companies suffering property damage. Fourteen Chinese activists decided to protest the purchase and protect China's sovereignty by sailing to the islands. Five landed on one of the Senkaku Islands, carrying the flags of China and Taiwan. These five plus the nine remaining on the boat were arrested by Japanese authorities. The Noda government immediately returned the activists to China, thus avoiding a potential political crisis, and activists received a hero's welcome. Four days later, ten Japanese activists reached one of the islands, waving Japanese flags. This prompted protest demonstrations in several Chinese cities with mobs attacking Japanese-made cars and Japanese businesses.

Japanese politicians reacted to the violence by proposing to place personnel on the islands to defend the sovereignty of the Senkakus and to assert "effective control" as defined in international law. The tension between the two countries reached a level where their militaries became involved. In December 2012, a Chinese military aircraft entered

Japanese airspace over the Senkaku Islands, and in subsequent months more Chinese fighter jets intruded into the airspace.[111]

Even before the flyover by Chinese aircrafts, large-scale intrusions by Chinese vessels into Japanese territorial waters were taking place. Early penetrations by Chinese fishing vessels were not minor accidents. They were planned operations, sometimes on a massive scale. In one incident, as many as one hundred Chinese fishing ships were involved. With civilian fishing vessels, the chances of violence are slim, but not so with naval ships. In June 2016, Chinese naval vessels entered the picture by intruding into Japan's contiguous zone around the Senkaku Islands for the first time. Maritime activities picked up. Two months after the naval intrusion, about two hundred to three hundred fishing vessels began operating in the vicinity of the islands, accompanied by Chinese Coast Guard and other government ships. Military aircraft were added to the mix, so there was now a volatile situation where harassment and even accidents could lead to armed conflict.

Coastal nations have a tendency to extend their territorial jurisdiction whenever there is an urgency to ensure their claims or to ward off potential competition from neighboring states. On February 25, 1992, China announced its "Law on the Territorial Sea and the Contiguous Zone." Article 2 of the law, for the first time, clearly states the Senkaku Islands belong to the People's Republic of China. In the other articles, Chinese sovereignty over its territorial sea and control over its contiguous zone is explained in detail. The contiguous zone extends control outward for 24 nm from the baseline. China controls not only the activities on the surface of the water but also the air space above and the subsoil underneath.

The dispute between Japan and China became contentious when both countries expanded their territorial sea beyond their contiguous zone by establishing their own Exclusive Economic Zone (EEZ), extending their territorial space an extra two hundred nautical miles. In May 1996, the PRC ratified the UNCLOS, and at the same time established its EEZ. China's EEZ is large because it follows the natural prolongation of its continental shelf as allowed by UNCLOS. The

---

111. Sheila A. Smith, *Intimate Rivals: Japanese Domestic Politics and a Rising China* (New York: Columbia University Press, 2015), 1-4.

Chinese claim their continental shelf extends out to what is known as the Okinawa Trough. In contrast, Japan measures its EEZ boundaries by the median line, which is equidistant from the territories of Japan and China. But even this seemingly equitable solution is fraught with controversy. How is the baseline defined? Without an agreed upon baseline, any measurement would be controversial. The width of the East China Sea, where the Senkaku Islands are located is only 360 nm between Chinese and Japanese territories. With Japan's EEZ extending 200 nm and China's EEZ extending almost 350 nm, there are serious EEZ overlaps. By declaring their EEZ, the countries not only control transit over the waters but also the mineral resources in the seabed beneath the ocean. The area around the Senkaku Islands is noted for its vast reserve of natural gas. When China began to drill for natural gas in the area, Japan protested because of the overlapping EEZ.

In November 2012, China extended its territorial jurisdiction by establishing the "East China Sea Air Defense Identification Zone" (East China Sea ADIZ). It was designed to deter foreign intrusion into Chinese air space and enforce the zone by whenever necessary "defensive emergency measures" of the Chinese Armed Forces. However, ADIZ is defined unilaterally by nation-states and is not enforceable by treaties or international organizations. Japan has a large ADIZ because of its numerous islands. It is not surprising that the Chinese announced ADIZ overlaps half of the Japanese ADIZ in the vicinity of the Senkaku Islands. Such overlapping creates the possibility of conflict, whether intentional or accidental.

Protecting sovereign rights is imperative. The other matter of importance is national security. National security concerns over the islands led the People's Republic of China to enact the Coast Guard Law (CGL) in January 2021. Up to this point, China used incremental steps to expand its control over disputed territories—slow, low-level coercion—sending several ships into contested zones and engaging in harassing movements. However, now the CGL authorizes the maritime law enforcement fleets to use lethal force on foreign ships in disputed waters. The use of militarized force to resolve conflict was immediately criticized by several countries. They said it is inconsistent with international law and in violation of UNCLOS. The CGL is ambiguous on the definition of maritime areas and how the rules governing the use of weapons are to be implemented. For China, the CGL meant better control over pending and future territorial disputes. The police force is the Coast Guard, which is under the People's Armed Police (PAP). Above the PAP in the organizational structure is the Central Military Committee, the highest national defense body. It is chaired by Xi Jinping, the head of the Chinese Communist Party and the supreme leader. The PAP is on the same level as the People's Liberation Army (PLA), the armed forces of the PRC.

It is believed the CGL was enacted to counter the increasing foreign intrusions around the Spratley Islands in the South China Sea. Up to the 1970s, there were no challenges to China's sovereignty over these islands. Then, the countries around the South China Sea—the Philippines, Vietnam, Taiwan, Indonesia, Malaysia, and Brunei began to claim some of the islands. What prompted these nations to put in their claims is the importance of the South China Sea as the main transit lane for ships traveling between the Pacific Ocean and the Indian Ocean through the Strait of Malacca. Just as important, if not more, is the rich fishing grounds and vast oil and natural gas reserves of this area.

What is unique about the Chinese response to these foreign challenges has been the building of artificial islands around the Spratly Islands. From December 2013 until October 2015, the Chinese built seven coral reefs into artificial islands, totaling about three thousand acres. Some are large enough for planes to land. China was not concerned about the severe ecological damage. Article 60 of the UNCLOS allows for the construction, operation and use of artificial islands.[112] However, China could be in violation of international law. The UNCLOS says, "States have the obligation to protect and preserve the marine environment."[113] There are other specific environmental provisions of UNCLOS that China seems to have violated. Even though heavily criticized, China has pushed ahead with aggressive military moves. If

---

112. UN Convention on the Law of the Sea, "Part 5: Exclusive Economic Zone," Article 60.

113. UN Convention on the Law of the Sea, "Part 12: Protection and Preservation of the Marine Environment," Section 1. General Provisions, Article 192.

this approach works successfully, it could be applied to the Senkaku dispute.

There have been some respites from this constant stream of confrontation. Fisheries agreements were negotiated between Japan and the PRC in 1975 and 1997. Both countries reached somewhat of a consensus in 2008 on the joint development of continental shelf resources but faced difficulties in implementation. Meanwhile, the PRC has been unilaterally developing the gas fields on their side of the boundary.[114]

The strategic location of the Senkaku Islands is of prime importance to all the major powers. The Senkakus are an integral part of the defense planning of Japan. With any hostilities in this region, the US is bound to come to the defense of Japan in accordance with the mutual security treaty. The US Seventh Fleet, with headquarters in Yokosuka, Japan, regularly patrols the East China Sea, helping to maintain an open shipping lane. From time to time, China has complained US naval ships from Yokosuka are violating China's territorial waters in the East China Sea. The US Navy has denied the Chinese complaints, saying its ships are always in international waters.Shipping lanes or sea freight lanes accessible in the East China Sea, and especially the adjoining South China Sea, are vital to several Indo-Pacific states. A great deal of traffic goes through these shipping routes. In addition to the issue of controlling the shipping lanes, the location of the islands allows it to serve as a base for power projection. The islands could work as a forward base for defense and, if necessary, could serve as a possible springboard for offensive actions.

---

114. Seokwoo Lee, ed., *Encyclopedia*, 108.

IMPLICATIONS

CHAPTER SIX

The two sets of major problems faced by Japan in the postwar period, constitutional and territorial, seem to be disparate. But when viewed from a long-range perspective, they are related and intertwined. The constitutional revision issues of the emperor and that of Article 9, when taken together, help to discern the foundations of Japan. Moreover, they affect how the territorial disputes are treated and, therefore, the direction taken.

The prewar planners had it right when they recommended the retention of the emperor and the imperial institution and included a pacifist clause to prevent Japan from engaging in a future war. The utmost importance of these two provisions is evident by their placement in the Constitution of Japan. After the preamble, starting with Article 1 and continuing to Article 8, the status and role of the emperor and that of the imperial institution are covered. It is followed by Article 9, assuring a peaceful, non-violent nation.

With importance comes controversy. Coming out of the disaster of the Pacific War, and the resulting chaos and deprivation, the majority wanted the emperor retained for the sake of stability and no more wars. A war renunciation clause was needed. General MacArthur and his staff were supporters of these provisions, for they knew the success of the Allied Occupation depended on the support and willingness of the Japanese people. The American drafters, with a little help from Japanese officials, made it a priority to have the two sets of innovative provisions at the head of the constitution.

Today, not all Japanese are willing to accept the emperor as merely a "symbol." Right-wing nationalists have a nostalgia for traditional Japan and want to expand the role of the emperor to make him a unifying force along the lines of the prewar concept of *kokutai* (national polity or national essence). There is no adequate English translation of this term; it is foreign to the Western world. *Kokutai* is a pseudo-religious doctrine that views Japan as more than a collection of people. Japan is a nation that transcends the people, and the emperor is the symbol of this transcendence—he is the embodiment of the Japanese people and the Japanese state. The nation is viewed as a family with the emperor as the head. The emperor comes from an unbroken line of descendants from the sun goddess, making the Japanese a unique and superior race. In prewar Japan, right-wing elements with strong nationalistic views used this rationale to legitimize militarism and the subjugation of neighboring countries. The concept of *kokutai* is antithetical to democracy because sovereignty lies with the emperor and not with the people; moreover, the emperor is a spiritual authority.

These sentiments still exist in a defused version of what it was in the 1930s and 1940s. Some extremists travel around in buses with loudspeakers broadcasting nationalistic messages. One prominent movement of the 1960s and 1970s was the Shield Society, a self-styled militia formed by the writer Yukio Mishima. Mishima believed in restoring political power to the emperor and the military. He criticized the US-imposed constitution for weakening the emperor, reducing him to a figurehead, and rendering the military weak by removing its ability to use force. Mishima and his Shield Society members believed the Western way of life was decadent, and that Japan needed to return to the traditional way of life. They believed a strong Japan was divinely chosen and protected. They attempted a coup at a military headquarters but failed when the cadets did not support them. Mishima committed seppuku, self-disembowelment by a short sword, better known as hara-kiri in the Western World. These right-wing groups, although vocal in expressing their nationalistic views, are a small minority and not a serious threat to change the status of the emperor or create an aggressive military force. Most Japanese today find the veneration of *kokutai* to be meaningless.

CONSERVATIVE STANCE

The traditional sentiments described above are not exclusively extreme right-wing. They are held in diluted form by some conservative leaders and persist in the psyche of traditionalists. Conservative thinking evolved over the years. It is important to see how their stance developed, its continuities and the changes that took place.

After the national election of 1946, the first election of the postwar era, Shigeru Yoshida became prime minister and served from the spring of 1946 through the spring of 1947 and for a second term from 1948 to 1954. For most of the Occupation, he was the prime minister and, therefore, the head of the Japanese government. He was influential in his opinion about the Constitution and the implementation of occupation policies. Yoshida was a staunch conservative, an advocate of the traditional way, and disdained some SCAP policies. He considered the policies too liberal and alien and tried to soften and delay their implementation.

Why would the Occupation work with such an individual? SCAP had few options. The basic decision was to use the indirect approach in the Occupation of Japan, wherein the Japanese leaders and personnel would carry out its policies. The political leadership consisted of old-line politicians and aristocrats. For these leaders, the emperor was sacrosanct. He was to be maintained and protected. These men held elitist attitudes. They believed the Japanese people were incapable of self-government, and it would take time to educate them in a democratic way. Individual freedom would be abused, so greater emphasis must be placed on individual responsibilities. These elitists were wedded to the Meiji Constitution, and when revisions were required, they thought only a few changes were necessary. For individuals like Joji Matsumoto, this meant almost no changes. He was unwilling to accept any new constitutional ideas. Prime Ministers Shidehara, Hatoyama, and Ishibashi were all reluctant to make major changes.

What caused the dramatic shift from the Meiji Constitution to the drafting of a new constitution were external pressures from the Allied powers and concern over domestic subversion and the rise of communism abroad. It affected the conservative stance. The change in Yoshida's thinking is instructive. His approach was pragmatic. Since

Japan had no armed forces, it was entirely dependent on the US military for its defense. This allowed the emphasis to be placed on economic recovery, not defense. During his second term as prime minister, US occupation policies changed radically. "Reverse course" took place, and the emphasis was on rapid economic development to strengthen Japan and ward off communist and other subversive threats. Japan was to meet these challenges by returning to the traditional bureaucratic and industrial elites to aid economic recovery.

In the beginning, Yoshida wanted to keep Article 9 intact because Japan was not ready to rearm and had to concentrate on economic development. He realized that once economic recovery had taken place, Japan may need to have a military force. This original stance of no constitutional reform, with an emphasis on economic development, became the so-called "Yoshida Doctrine." According to this view, there are three main pillars: security through alliance with the US, minimal military armaments and spending, and an emphasis on economic growth and recovery. But Yoshida never talked about a "doctrine," and the Japanese government did not issue any such documents or announcements. The Yoshida Doctrine is an analytical construct created by academics to describe and justify postwar Japanese foreign policy. It was introduced in the 1970s and was widely used until the 1990s. Even today, the Yoshida Doctrine is used by experts to describe Japanese foreign policy of the early postwar period. Explaining Japanese support for demilitarization is not so simple because many political leaders were ambivalent. Although Yoshida supported Article 9 with its restrictions on the use of military force, he admitted in the future, Japan may have to resort to rearmament. Furthermore, successful economic recovery and growth were assumed to be linked to reduced defense expenditures. However, recent studies have shown that reduced defense spending does not equate to increased economic growth. Economic growth was due to other factors, and defense spending played a minor role. Nevertheless, moderate conservative leaders used the Yoshida Doctrine as the basis of their rationale and followed it until the end of the Cold War.[115]

When the LDP was formed in November 1955, it brought together a variety of political ideologies, but the party is best described as the political right. The faction led by Ichiro Hatoyama (prime minister from 1954-56) denounced the Yoshida Doctrine and supported remilitarization, but it was kept in check and unable to control the LDP. Under the premiership of Hayato Ikeda (1960-1964), the Yoshida Doctrine was enshrined as the pivotal point of Japan's postwar policies. Ikeda founded the Kochikai (Broad Pond Society), which became a leading faction in the LDP, producing five prime ministers. The Kochikai is a moderate faction on domestic and foreign policy issues, noted for following the Yoshida Doctrine with an emphasis on pacifism, economic growth, and close relations with the US.But even Ikeda realized remilitarization could not be stopped. It could only be temporarily delayed until public opinion eventually supported it.[116]

The prime ministers that followed Ikeda—Masayoshi Ohira, Zenko Suzuki, and Kiichi Miyazawa—had similar political views. They placed emphasis on economic development, alliance with the US, and preservation of the pacifist constitution. Clearly, they were adherents of the Yoshida Doctrine. But Ikeda, Ohira, and even Yoshida were flexible and believed Japan should not be totally dependent on the US in regard to self-defense and were open to rearmament.[117]

With the end of the Cold War, changes occurred in how constitutional revision and militarization were viewed. New regional challenges affected the international position of Japan. Japan first started with peacekeeping and humanitarian missions promoted by the UN. As a major economic power, Japan wanted to exercise its role as a responsible partner in the world community. SDF contingents

---

115. Hiroyuki Hoshio, "Deconstructing the 'Yoshida Doctrine,'" *Japanese Journal of Political Science* 23, Issue 2 (June 2022): 105-28; Yoneyuki Sugita, "The Yoshida Doctrine as a Myth," *The Japanese Journal of American Studies*, no. 27 (2016): 123-43. Both articles are critical of the Yoshida Doctrine.

116. Karol Zakowski, "Kochikai of the Japanese Liberal Democratic Party and Its Evolution After the Cold War," *The Korean Journal of International Studies* 9, no. 2 (December 2011): 183-84.

117. Zakowski, "Kochikai," 187.

were sent abroad to many nations. At the same time, nationalistic ideas gradually became more popular as tensions built up in the Middle East and East Asia. The turning point came in 2001. The war on terrorism and the Gulf War caused Japan to be involved in international efforts to resolve these serious threats. But it also raised the question of what Japan's contribution should be. The Koizumi government did not send SDF to help in Operation Desert Storm, but it did send military personnel to Iraq in a controversial move. Meanwhile, in East Asia, Chinese vessels began to intrude into the waters around the Senkaku Islands, and China aggressively claimed the islands. North Korea started missile and nuclear testing and made hostile statements. After a hiatus of several years, these developments revived the national debate on the amendment of Article 9. Presently, there is still some doubt about changing Article 9 among the leaders of the Kochikai, the leading faction of the LDP. But undeniably, there is a departure from the Yoshida Doctrine.

In the twenty-first century, the geopolitical scene in Northeast Asia was altered drastically by the rise of Chinese economic influence and the expansion of its military power. Domestic politics was affected by Japanese politicians in a state of flux, debating how to handle the disputes with neighbors and to what degree it should defend its sovereignty. A breakthrough from the usual low-posture approach came with the premiership of two individuals with the longest tenure in postwar Japan, Junichiro Koizumi from 2001 to 2006 and Shinzo Abe from 2006 to 2007 and 2012 to 2020. This was unusual because previously Japan's prime minister had changed virtually every year. Koizumi served for five years and Abe for nine years. It appears sufficient time in the office is necessary to launch a substantial program or at least have a long-range vision.

If Koizumi's LDP Draft of 2005 or Abe's LDP Draft of 2012 were enacted, they would have provided the necessary changes in Article 9 to legitimize the SDF as a military force. The proposals would have provided the SDF with the capabilities to undertake collective security measures with its allies, to participate in peacekeeping, and other global missions. But even with these provisions, the LDP would have faced formidable challenges in keeping its factions and coalition partners and most importantly, garnering sufficient popular support. The overseas deployment in UN peacekeeping, the Gulf War, and the Afghan and Iraq wars all faced opposition, and public opinion especially frustrated the ambitious plans of Koizumi and Abe.

To gain the support of the Japanese people, the political leadership has to show positive results in its management of disputes with neighboring countries, particularly China, or at the least improve the situation. In 2009, Japanese voters chose a new party to lead the country, the Democratic Party of Japan (DPJ), but the DPJ could not settle the 2010 trawler crisis with China and soon lost its power to rule. Disillusionment with the political parties and their leadership was expressed in declining approval in public opinion polls.

Even though the public has been dissatisfied with the political parties, developments abroad moved the conservative leaders to continue their push for Article 9 revision. Prime Minister Kishida promised to continue the legacy of Abe by successfully amending some portions of Article 9. He heads the Kochikai faction, known for its moderate stance. Kishida is more comfortable with a consensus, slow-moving approach, a departure from Abe's confrontational style. It has taken some seven decades to reach this point. At an opportune time when the public had gravitated toward a more open view of Article 9, the LDP should be able to pass a narrow, single-item revision.

NATIONALISM, MILITARISM AND INTERNATIONAL POLITICS

Contest over islands has become a question of national identity and global influence. Let us first examine the matter of national identity. When a nation claims an island or a set of islands, it places its name on that territory. The islands belong to that nation; it owes every inch, and it does not matter if it is small and uninhabited or a mere rock sticking out of the ocean. National pride is evoked, and people will defend the island. This is territorial nationalism, an emotional force in domestic politics. Citizens can be easily mobilized to protect their territory. The stakes are raised, and so much emotion is involved that compromise is difficult. If the territory is yours, why should you compromise?

What happens when another country adamantly claims the same island? The final solution is to go to war. And this is what happened with the Falklands Islands. The Falkland Islands are part of the overseas territory of the United Kingdom and have been under British rule since 1833. Argentina, which has its own name for the islands, Las Malvinas, claimed the islands because it inherited them from the Spanish crown in the early nineteenth century. Also, the islands are in closer proximity to Argentina. Argentina invaded the islands in 1982 with patriotic fervor but was defeated by the British. Today, the Falklands remain under British sovereignty, but Argentina still maintains its claim.

If sovereignty cannot be resolved, the resources of the islands could be shared, and transit around and over the islands could be worked out and, thereby bypassing the sovereignty issue. On the three territorial small islands covered in this book, disputes are under discussion, negotiations have taken place, and on occasion, fisheries and natural resources exploration and extraction agreements have been worked out, but there are many gaps remaining. Joint exploration and access to gas, oil, and minerals have proven to be more difficult due to the value of the resources and problems in delimiting boundaries. Unfortunately, when negotiation and diplomacy break down, harsh statements are exchanged, and sometimes coercive pressure is applied. Aggressive demands and counter-demands could lead to military probes with the likelihood of accidents or miscalculations taking place, leading to inadvertent clashes.

Negotiations have been troubled by memories of the past—the past will not die. The Republic of Korea (ROK) and the People's Republic of China (PRC) have continually evoked the legacy of the past in their negotiations, reminding the Japanese of the brutal treatment of their citizens by the Japanese military. The ROK mentions the demeaning colonial policies, comfort women (sexual slavery), and compensation issues, while the PRC cites the cruel wartime practices of the Japanese army and compensation difficulties. Even though there are few survivors, bitter memories are aroused, and the past experiences are passed on to succeeding generations.

The legacy of the past includes the visits to the Yasukuni Shrine by Japanese leaders. The government established Yasukuni Shrine as a repository for the spirits of Japan's war dead, who died fighting for their country in the name of the emperor. The Occupation ended State

Shinto, the joining of state and religion, but it did not stop the effort to memorialize Japan's war dead. In 1978, fourteen Japanese Class A war criminals were enshrined at Yasukuni. This outraged the Japanese public, and Yasukuni and its supporters were severely criticized.China and Korea protested the enshrinement. Many Japanese consider the Yasukuni Shrine a symbol of a disgraced military past. For Chinese, Koreans, and other Asians who suffered under Japanese occupation and colonial rule, bitter memories are evoked by dignitaries visiting Yasukuni.

Emperor Hirohito visited Yasukuni eight times between 1945 and 1975 but probably stopped visiting the shrine because of the enshrined war criminals. His son, Akihito, and the current emperor, Naruhito, have never visited the shrine. In the postwar period, many Japanese prime ministers paid their respects at Yasukuni, but they did it privately, not in an official capacity. The first visit by a prime minister that sparked domestic and international controversy was by Yasuhiro Nakasone and his cabinet on the fortieth anniversary of the war's end. It was heavily criticized by the Chinese and led to mass protests. The relationship between Japan and China deteriorated when Koizumi insisted on annual visits from 2001 to 2006. Seven years later, Abe, who tried to improve relations with China, visited the shrine in December 2013.It caused an uproar not only in Beijing but in Seoul as well. Abe did not go again, as it was not worth the political cost. Domestically, Yasukuni Shrine continues to be a contentious issue between conservative nationalists who seek to honor those who died fighting for Japan and postwar liberals who argue for the separation of state and religion and the protection of popular sovereignty as provided in Japan's Constitution.

Concurrent with the anxiety over Japan's past behavior is the fear of the current rise of Japanese militarism. Neighboring countries recognize this in the increasing size, capabilities, and functions of the SDF. But from Japan's point of view, the increase in defense spending is a response to the changing balance of power in Northeast Asia. The expanding military power of China and North Korea has created unease over the inadequacy of Japan's defenses. In addition, the failure of peaceful negotiations to resolve the island disputes has added urgency to revise Article 9. Russia's invasion of Ukraine gave rise to fear of possible aggressive actions by the Russians towards the Northern Territories. These developments have moved the public to support an increase in armed forces and a more defined mission of defending the country.

If negotiations and other diplomatic moves fail, and nations do not want to resort to armed conflict, what other approaches are there? International law and conventions have not been helpful because of conflicting definitions and interpretations. Differing baselines have skewed the maritime boundaries in the East China Sea. China uses a straight baseline, whereas Japan does not. If there is no agreement on the baseline, it throws into question how far a country's boundaries extend. There are serious overlaps between China's claim of the natural prolongation of the continental shelf and Japan's expansive EEZ. Where are the boundaries? In a joint mining operation, which side of the perceived boundary do you start? Furthermore, intrusions by ships and aircraft into conflicting zones create irritating problems.

Third-party adjudicators or arbitrators could be used to resolve some of the issues. However, the parties involved have to agree on the method of dispute resolution. A binding decision is often made based on international law. None of the three countries in this study would consent to this approach. The territorial disputes are too complex, and there are few case laws on sovereignty using this method. If there is a possibility of utilizing a third party, it would be a court—the International Court of Justice (ICJ) in The Hague. The ICJ has adjudicated territorial disputes, and a considerable body of international case law has emerged about sovereignty issues such as boundaries and baseline delineation. The parties must agree to take the dispute to the ICJ, but such an agreement does not seem possible. China cites the ICJ as a Western institution skewed to favor Western nations. Since the US has a defense treaty with Japan, it is involved in the Senkaku issue. Beijing fears the ICJ would favor Japan as an ally of the US. Both China and Japan want to avoid being on the losing side in a court case—the stakes are too high to take the risk. Whichever government loses the Senkakus, would be humiliated and face severe domestic criticism. On the matter of Dokdo, Japan is willing to refer the Dokdo dispute to ICJ, but South Korea refuses on the grounds that it already has sovereignty over the islands and there is nothing to decide. It is an untenable position, and the ROK has come under criticism. As for the Northern Territories, Russia and Japan want to avoid the ICJ. They feel negotiations, although unsuccessful so far, are still the route to take. Both countries are content to defer the resolution of the dispute for another time.

What makes the negotiations difficult is the concern over global influence. Of all the islands, the Senkaku Islands stand out for its strategic importance. Apart from the value of the rich resources surrounding the area—its oil, natural gas, minerals, and fishing—the islands are located in the vital transit lanes of the East China Sea. In addition, the Senkakus are in close proximity to Taiwan, some 90 nm away. Beijing believes that the US and Japan are trying to prevent the unification of Taiwan with China. The uniting of Taiwan with China is, of course, a major goal of the Beijing government. Taken as a whole, the East China Sea and the adjoining South China Sea are part of the hegemonic plan of the PRC. China already plays a dominant role in the South China Sea and wants to extend its control northward into the East China Sea.

All the island disputes are linked together. For instance, if Japan were to relinquish its claim to the Northern Territories, it would weaken its position with Dokdo and the Senkaku Islands. This will have a domino effect. For China, to give in to Japan on the Senkakus weakens its claim to all the Spratly Islands in the South China Sea. Perception is critical, and China is determined to project a strong image of resolutely pursuing and defending its territorial policies.

Although all three territorial island disputes have evoked hostility between the countries, there are differences in the degree and nature of the conflicts. The island problems began with the occupation of the entire Kuril chain of islands by the Soviet troops and the eviction of their Japanese residents. The dispute over the Northern Territories has been at the governmental level and few citizens have participated in protests. Over the years, there were few infringements of territorial space and no military confrontations. Conflict has been held in abeyance, but in recent years, there has been an expansion of Russian military capabilities with the introduction of new weapon systems.

The last of the territorial island disputes, the Senkaku Island, occurred twenty-five years after the Northern Territories issue began, but today, it is volatile with the greatest potential for conflict. Protests have been at both the government and public levels. Moreover, military units are involved. There have been frequent penetration of Japanese water and air spaces by government and private vessels and by military planes. With harassment and the show of force, there is greater risk of miscalculations and accidents occurring and leading to armed conflict.

Dokdo seems to have the best chance of being resolved. Government officials have made their claims, while the public has engaged in mass demonstrations. Except for a small military detachment stationed in Dokdo, there is no military involvement. Encroachment of territorial water and air space has not been a problem. There are other factors that could help to resolve the problem. Both South Korea and Japan have defense alliances with the US and, therefore, are allies. They are trading partners, and their economies are intertwined. The growth of Chinese power in Northeast Asia is a concern, and they have sovereignty problems with China—Japan and China claim the Senkaku Islands, while South Korea and China claim the Ieodo Reef.[118] With China as a common foe, Japan and South Korea have a reason to come together in defense against China. A bigger reason for Japan and the ROK joining together in defense is North Korea's nuclear and missile threats. The US has worked with Japan and South Korea in a cooperative move to block North Korea's advancing nuclear and missile arsenal. On August 18, 2023, President Joe Biden, Prime Minister Fumio Kishida, and South Korean President Yoon Suk Yeol met at Camp David, Maryland, in a trilateral summit; this was the first time the three countries had met for such a meeting. Although the focus was on North Korea, there were also mutual concerns about China's pursuit of domination in East Asia. Agreements made included the establishment of a "crisis hotline," a statement reaffirming the "peace and stability" across the Taiwan Strait, expanding joint maneuvers, sharing intelligence, and plans to meet

---

118. Ieodo (in Korean) or Suyan (in Chinese) is also known as Socotra Rock (in English). It is a submerged rock located in the Yellow Sea. According to the UNCLOS, a submerged reef cannot be claimed as territory by any country. Nevertheless, South Korea and China have claimed it as part of their EEZ. Ieodo is 149 km from the nearest Korean island and 245 km from the nearest Chinese island.

regularly. As Japan and the ROK seek deeper security cooperation, it could spin off another issue and lead to a broad agreement on access and development of resources around Dokdo, thus circumventing the thorny sovereignty claims to the islands. The possibility of submitting the dispute to the ICJ is there, but the ROK will have to tone down the nationalistic fervor. The benefits of forging a bond of friendship and cooperation should far outweigh the loss of a couple of islets, but intense emotions are involved. South Korea has a strong case and should be willing to take the risk.

The last resort is to apply militarized force to solve the problem. China seems to be moving in that direction. By enacting the Coast Guard Law in 2021, Beijing allowed the use of lethal force to defend its sovereignty rights. Chinese naval vessels, including missile-equipped destroyers, have plowed through the waters of the Senkakus in increasing numbers, and jet aircraft have flown regularly near the islands. The planes are used not only for reconnaissance and surveillance but for harassment.

In Japan, the increasing use of the military has been opposed by pacifist organizations. As previously stated, the pacifist movement has declined, but it still remains a potent force in domestic politics. Polls show a sizable number of Japanese are against remilitarization and the use of the military in an offensive capacity. The movement is an emotional force, as seen in the annual observance on the anniversary of the atomic bombing of Hiroshima and Nagasaki. A visit to the Hiroshima Peace Memorial Museum is a visual reminder of the horrors of war, so much so that officials had to remove exhibits because they were seriously disturbing and affecting some visitors.

Other groups have joined in protesting the alteration of Article 9. Women's rights and labor rights groups, for example, opposed the reform of Article 9, fearing it could be the start of wholesale revision of the constitution that would affect their enshrined rights.

With rising militarism, the tendency is to seek military solutions. But the cost is great, and states want to avoid armed conflict as much as possible. Therefore, diplomacy and negotiations remain the best ways to avoid conflict. Contradictory historical documents, confusing international standards and precedents, and ambiguous international laws are not the main obstacles to resolving disputes. The main culprit is national pride. Territorial nationalism is a potent emotional force. Citizens are ready to defend any piece of rock, even to die if necessary. Such nationalistic passions make small island disputes an almost impossible task to solve. Not only is the political leadership involved, but the populace as well. It would take some time for nationalistic fervor to subside. Small island disputes have persisted for a long time, and the immediate prospect of resolution is not in sight.

AMERICAN INVOLVEMENT

This book began with a description of how the United States with prewar and wartime planning, prepared for the handling of postwar Japan. American planning continued after the war; in fact, it intensified with the Occupation, which turned out to be solely an American operation. Americans drafted the Constitution and overlooked the implementation and administration of reform policies. The Japanese had a minor role in the writing of the Constitution and a larger role in administering the occupation policies, but it was always under the guise of SCAP supervision.

The San Francisco Peace Treaty ended the Occupation, and Japan regained its sovereignty, but this did not diminish American influence in Japan's defense planning. Instead, the US presence in Japan was solidified under the US-Japan Security Treaty, whereby the US was allowed to have its military personnel stationed on bases in Japan. This arrangement, known as the San Francisco System, was a win-win for both parties. Japan was defenseless without an armed force and needed a security guarantee.

The US was concerned about Soviet and Chinese Communist aggressive moves, and with the outbreak of the Korean War, there was a need for forward bases in Northeast Asia. These bases would serve as jumping points to deter communist advances. Therefore, the security treaty provided the immediate defensive needs of both countries. To this day, the treaty continues to be the basis for Japan's foreign and defense policies. Without a major breakdown in seventy years, the San Francisco System has been a success for both countries. The security treaty also played a part, though not dominant, in the rapid economic recovery of Japan.

There were, however, negative consequences that need to be considered. The security treaty lessened the independence of Japan and made it a willing junior partner in US Cold War policies. There were a number of episodes where Washington pressured Japan to follow its lead. The Japanese word for such pressure is *gaiatsu* (foreign pressure). After the peace conference, the US used *gaiatsu* to force Japan into signing the Sino-Japan Peace Treaty of 1952 with the ROC (Taiwan), thereby recognizing the ROC as the legitimate government of China. In a letter to John Foster Dulles, Prime Minister Yoshida said Japan intends to sign a treaty with the ROC, but he discreetly did not mention that his government was reluctant.[119] It was a move Japan would not have made because it did not want to antagonize its close neighbor, the PRC. Many Japanese did not want a strained relationship with China, and certainly the business community was not pleased.

The San Francisco Peace Treaty did not mention Okinawa since it was assumed to be part of Japan Proper. Okinawa and the rest of the Ryukyu chain became a vital part of US military planning. It was essentially an American military fortress, a key staging area for military operations. During the Korean War, bombing missions were carried out from Kadena Air Force base in Okinawa, and in the Vietnam War, air attacks were launched against North Vietnam, Cambodia, and Laos from the same base. Japanese officials and the general public found it disconcerting to have Japan indirectly involved in the Korean and Vietnam wars. Several felt Japan was complicit in supporting American military actions in Asia.

At the end of the Occupation, the US retained administrative control over Okinawa and the Ryukyu Islands chain, with only "residual sovereignty" granted to Japan. Okinawans protested the confiscation of land, the extensive use of land for military purposes, noise pollution, environmental degradation, and GI crimes that are inevitable with the establishment of large military bases. That these problems arose from the stationing of foreign troops did not make it easier for the Japanese

---

119. *https://worldjpn.net* > texts > JPCH.

government. It continues to be an irritant in Okinawa, where about three-fourths of US military personnel are stationed.

There are two major concerns the Japanese government has in its political and military relations with the US. First, the fear of entrapment. There are apprehensions that Japan will be drawn into prolonged conflicts due to its alliance with the US. Two examples would be the Korean and Vietnam wars. Some of the wars may initially be successful, such as Afghanistan and Iraq, but could turn into protracted warfare. In Afghanistan, it lasted for twenty years. These wars are not in the national interest of Japan; they are of peripheral concern. Japan's principal interest is to safeguard its territory. The second fear is ensuring total control of its command. Japan is in an unequal power relationship, so it has to maintain its ability to make strategic decisions and not be presented with a fait accompli. This means consultations at the highest levels.

Regarding the territorial island disputes, the US was and is involved in all of them. In handling these disputes, the US always considered its strategic needs first. The US supported Japan's position only when it coincided with its own strategic priorities. At the Yalta conference, the US and Britain secretly decided to "hand over" the Kuril Islands to the Soviet Union as an inducement for the Soviets to declare war against Japan. Roosevelt made the bargain with Stalin, and Churchill had to go along. This use of the Kurils to help hasten the end of the war has been described as a "bargaining chip" by the political scientist Kimie Hara. At the end of the war, the Soviets hurriedly occupied all of the Kurils, even the four islands near Hokkaido, which they had never before claimed nor had any kind of jurisdiction. Japan only wanted the four southernmost islands in the Kurils because of their proximity to Hokkaido and the long history of settlements by the Japanese.

The US changed its position in the midst of the Cold War, and by the time the peace conference in San Francisco occurred, the US had decided the disputed islands were Japanese territory under Soviet military occupation. The peace treaty neither assigned the Kurils to the Soviet Union nor mentioned the four islands. In the ensuing years, American and Japanese planners concluded that the two small and southernmost islands were an inherent part of Japan and the other two larger islands could be considered part of Russian-held Kuril islands. In the peace treaty negotiations with the Soviet Union in 1956, the Soviets offered the "two island return" solution, and initially, the Japanese accepted. But Secretary of State John Foster Dulles informed the Japanese foreign minister that if Japan accepted the two islands return, and ceded sovereign rights to the two larger islands, the US would be entitled to "full sovereignty over the Ryukyus." The pressure was on, and Japan rejected the two islands return solution. Here, the US determined the final outcome. If the US had not intervened, Japan's acceptance of the offer would have ended the dispute. In the Cold War competition with the Soviet Union, it was in the interest of the US to stop Soviet expansionism. The Soviet Union pushed back and withdrew its offer. Although diplomatic relations resumed between the two countries, the peace treaty was never signed.[120]

The US had a hand in the Dokdo dispute, although it was a passive and vacillating role. In the early drafts of the peace treaty, American planners clearly recognized Dokdo as part of Korea. But in December 1949, right after the establishment of the PRC, US planners changed their position and assigned Dokdo to Japan. After the Korean War started in June 1950, the draft treaties no longer mentioned Takeshima. The final peace treaty vaguely references Korean independence and does not specifically mention Takeshima. A month before the San Francisco Peace Conference, the US notified the South Korean government that it considered Dokdo to be under Japanese sovereignty. If the US had Japan's interest in mind, it would have inserted Dokdo into the peace treaty as part of Japan, ending the dispute over the islands. But the US thought only about its own strategic interest. Consequently, the dispute continued over the years, as the US took a hands-off policy. The US did not want to damage the mutual security defense pact it had with each country. Both countries were encouraged to settle their differences, but the question of territorial claim was set aside.

The US signed the Okinawa Reversion Agreement in 1971, and it went into effect in 1972, returning sovereignty over Okinawa to Japan.

---

120. For background information on the three territorial island disputes, see Kimie Hara, *Cold War Frontiers in the Asia-Pacific: Divided Territories in the San Francisco System* (New York: Routledge, 2007). There are separate chapters for each dispute—chapter one on Dokdo, chapter three on Northern Territories, and chapter seven on the Senkakus.

The Senkakus were included as part of the Ryukyu and belonged to Japan. The PRC and even the ROC did not strenuously protest. In the 1970s, when the importance of the Senkakus was realized, the PRC and the ROC pushed their claims to the islands. The US is indirectly involved because it is obligated as an alliance partner to come to the defense of Japan. In addition, due to the proximity of the Senkakus to Taiwan, both Japan and the US are concerned about the forceful return of Taiwan to China. Such a unification would reinforce Beijing's claim of sovereignty over the Senkaku Island and expand its influence over the entire East China Sea. It would be a threat to American and Japanese interests. Japan and the US are inextricably bonded, and Japan has become a participant in American military policies in Asia.

Though American influence in the territorial disputes has played an important part, it is in defense planning that the US has the most pronounced impact. Americans planned and helped implement Article 9. Although there is some ambiguity as to who initially placed the article in the draft constitution, it is undeniable that the US was the impetus for seeking permanent disarmament. The Japanese leaders understood Article 9 prohibited any rearmament, even in the name of self-defense. Abrupt changes occurred with the perceived threat of communism and the start of the Korean War. Even before the outbreak of the war, the US was pressuring the Japanese government to rearm. John Foster Dulles made a special trip to Tokyo, and part of his plan was to ask Japan to rearm. Yoshida balked at the suggestion, but the start of the Korean War quickly ended the discussion. Tokyo and Washington knew this was unconstitutional but was a beneficial and strategic move. The ambiguous wording of Article 9 provided a way out, and both American and Japanese planners took advantage of it. What they did not expect was strong popular opposition to any attempt to revise Article 9. Efforts to remilitarize were stymied by the inability to pass any constitution revision bill. The Japanese government found a way around this blockage by the method called "revision by interpretation." Slowly, step-by-step, the size of the SDF was increased, capabilities enhanced, and the role it played expanded.

Japan was slow in responding to the US exertion in global missions, especially US-led missions. When Japan offered a token financial contribution, it was severely criticized by its allies. But surprisingly, when there is less US pressure, the Japanese public is more willing to support SDF missions abroad. For example, their support of sending noncombat SDF units to Afghanistan. Since the hawkish premiership of Koizumi and Abe, Japan has expanded its military capabilities to project force well beyond its borders. It has done this even without broad popular support. Today, Japan can participate much more actively in collective self-defense with the US.

All of this comes at a huge cost. It is more than the commitment of large financial resources—it also involves political and social costs. There is an impact on the way decisions are made and policies carried out. Are the decisions on Article 9 in accord with the majority views of the Japanese public? One immediate question arises. Does increasing militarization make Japan more secure, or does it place Japan in greater danger? China and North Korea view Japan as a potential threat and have undertaken defensive moves. Preemptive strikes are part of their defensive strategy. Even distant Asian countries have memories of Japan as a threat to their security. Japan has taken great measures to assure its neighbors that it is primarily concerned with maintaining peace and stability in East Asia. However, historical memories are stirred by Japan's move toward greater militarization. It could affect trade relations and impact other exchanges with neighboring countries.

What has been sketched out are two broad paths of development in terms of Japan's security and its role in world politics. First, there are those who want to see Japan as a powerful political and military player, which would be in line with its role as a major economic power. Changes in the power position of China and North Korea have undermined Japan's security, so constitutional revisions need to reflect this reality. Then, there are those who say Japan has done well in avoiding conflicts with other countries. Although the situation in East Asia has become tense, there is no need to exacerbate the situation by wholesale rearming. A minor fine-tuning of the Japanese Constitution is all that is required. So, we return to the original questions—what direction should Japan take, and what role should it play in the global community?

BIBLIOGRAPHY

Auer, James E. "Article Nine of Japan's Constitution: From Renunciation of Armed Force 'Forever' to the Third Largest Defense Budget in the World," *Law and Contemporary Problems* 53, no. 2 (Winter/Spring, 1990): 171-87.

Barnes, Dayna L. *Architects of Occupation: American Experts and Planning for Postwar Japan.* Ithaca, NY: Cornell University Press, 2017.

Barrash, Ike. "Russia's Militarization of the Kuril Islands." Center for Strategic and International Studies (September 27, 2022).

Beauchamp, Edward R. *History of Contemporary Japan, 1945-1998.* Edited by Edward R. Beauchamp. New York: Garland Publishing, 1998.

Behr, Edward S. *Hirohito: Behind the Myth.* New York: Villard Books, 1989.

Bergamini, David. *Japan's Imperial Conspiracy: How Emperor Hirohito Led Japan into War Against the West.* New York: William Morrow, 1971.

Berkofsky, Axel. *A Pacifist Constitution for an Armed Empire: Past and Present of Japanese Security and Defence Policies.* Milan: Franco Angeli, 2012.

Bix, Herbert P. *Hirohito and the Making of Modern Japan.* New York: Harper Collins Publisher, 2000.

Borton, Hugh. *American Presurrender Planning for Postwar Japan.* New York: East Asian Institute, Columbia University, 1967.

Borton, Hugh. *Spanning Japan's Modern Century: The Memoirs of Hugh Borton.* Lanham, MD: Lexington Books, 2002.

Bowman, Garret. "Why Now is the Time to Resolve the Dokdo/Takeshima Dispute," *Case Western Reserve Journal of International Law* 46, issue 1 (Fall 2013): 433-62.

Cho, Jinman, HeeMin Kim, and Jun Young Choi. "The Dokdo/Takeshima Dispute between Korea and Japan: Understanding the Whole Picture," *Pacific Focus* 24, no. 3 (December 2009): 365-78.

Cohen, Theodore and Herbert Passin. *Remaking Japan.* New York: The Free Press, 1987.

Craig, William. *The Fall of Japan: The Final Weeks of World War II in the Pacific.* New York: Dial Press, 1967.

Cummings, Bruce. *The Origins of the Korean War, Vol. 1: Liberation and the Emergence of Separate Regimes, 1945-1947.* Princeton, NJ: Princeton University Press, 1981.

da Silva, Diego Lopes, Xiao Jiang, Lorenzo Scarazzato, Lucie Beraud-Sudreau, Ana Assis, and Nan Tian. "Trends in World Military Expenditures, 2022." *Stockholm International Peace Research Institute Fact Sheet.* Stockholm: SIPRI, April 2023, https://doi.org/10.55163/PNVP2622.

de Bary, Wm. Theodore, ed. *Sources of Japanese Tradition.* New York: Columbia University Press, 1958.

Department of State. *A Decade of American Policy: 1941-1949, Basic Documents.* Washington, DC: Historical Office, Department of State, 1950, 28-40.

Department of State. *Foreign Relations of the United States, 1946.* Washington, DC: Government Printing Office, 8:99-102.

Department of State. *Foreign Relations of the United States, 1951.* Washington, DC: Government Printing Office, 6:1206.

Department of State. *Postwar Foreign Policy Preparation, 1939-1945.* Washington, DC: Government Printing Office, 1949, 67-213.

Department of State. *Treaties and Other International Agreements of the United States of America, 1776-1949.* Washington, DC: Government Printing Office, 1969, 858.

deVillafranca, Richard. "Japan and the Northern Territories Dispute: Past, Present, Future," *Asian Survey* 33, no. 6 (June 1993): 610-24.

Dobbs, Charles M. *The Unwanted Symbol: American Foreign Policy, the Cold War, and Korea, 1945-1950.* Kent, OH: Kent State University Press, 1981.

Dower, John W. *Embracing Defeat: Japan in the Wake of World War II.* New York: W. W. Norton, 1999.

Dower, John W. *Empire and Aftermath: Yoshida Shigeru and the Japanese Experience, 1878-1954.* Harvard East Asian Monographs, September 15, 1988.

Dower, John W. "The San Francisco System: Past, Present, Future in U.S.-Japan-China Relations," *The Asia-Pacific Journal* 12, issue 8, no. 2 (February 23, 2014).

Dudden, Alexis. *Troubled Apologies Among Japan, Korea, and the United States.* New York: Columbia University Press, 2008.

Feis, Herbert. *Churchill, Roosevelt, Stalin: The War They Waged and the Peace They Sought.* Princeton, NJ: Princeton University Press, 1957.

Finn, Richard B. *Winners in Peace: MacArthur, Yoshida, and Postwar Japan.* Berkeley: University of California Press, 1992.

Foreign Ministry of Japan, Treaties Bureau. *Heiwa joyaku no teiketsu ni kansuru choso,* 7:267-84.

Fukui, Haruhiro. "Twenty Years of Revisionism." In Henderson, *The Constitution of Japan,* 41-70.

Genova, Alexandra. "Two Nations Disputed These Small Islands for 300 Years." *National Geographic* (November 14, 2018),

Gordon, Beate Sirota. *The Only Women in the Room: A Memoir of Japan, Human Rights, and the Arts.* Chicago: University of Chicago Press, 1997.

Hara, Kimie. *Cold War Frontiers in the Asia-Pacific: Divided Territories in the San Francisco System.* New York: Routledge, 2007.

Hara, Kimie. *Japanese-Soviet/Russian Relations Since 1945: A Difficult Peace.* New York: Routledge, 1998.

Hata, Ikuhiko. "Japan Under the Occupation," *The Japan Interpreter* 10, nos. 2-4 (Winter 1976): 361-80.

Hellegers, Dale M. *We, the Japanese People: World War II and the Origins of the Japanese Constitution.* 2 vols. Stanford: Stanford University Press, 2001.

Henderson, Dan Fenno, ed. *The Constitution of Japan: Its First Twenty Years, 1947-67.* Seattle: University of Washington Press, 1968.

Higuchi, Yoichi. "The Constitution and the Emperor System: Is Revisionism Alive?" *Law and Contemporary Problems* 53, no. 1 (Winter 1990): 51-60.

Hook, Glenn D. and Gavan McCormack. *Japan's Contested Constitution: Documents and Analysis.* NewYork: Routledge, 2001.

Hoshino, Hiroyuki. "Deconstructing the 'Yoshida Doctrine,'" *Japanese Journal of Political Science* 23, issue 2 (June 2022): 105-28.

Inoue, Kyoko. *MacArthur's Japanese Constitution: A Linguistic and Cultural Study of its Making.* Chicago: University of Chicago Press, 1991.

Iriye, Akira. "Continuities in U.S.-Japanese Relations, 1941-49." In Nagai and Iriye, *The Origins of the Cold War in Asia*, 378-407.

Ishizuka, Nobuhisa. "Constitutional Reform in Japan," *Columbia Journal of Asian Law* 33, no. 1 (2019): 5-40.

Ito, Hirobumi. *Commentaries on the Constitution of the Empire of Japan.* Translated by Miyoji Ito. 3rd ed. Tokyo: Chuo-o Daigaku, 1931.

Kades, Charles L. "The American Role in Revising Japan's Imperial Constitution," *Political Science Quarterly* 104, no. 2 (1989): 215-47.

Kawagishi, Norikazu. "The Constitution of Japan: An Unfinished Revolution." J.S.D. Dissertation, Yale Law School, 2003.

Keene, Donald. *The Japanese Discovery of Europe: Honda Toshiaki and Other Discoverers, 1720-1798.* London: Routledge and Kegan Paul, 1952.

Kim, Pilkyu. *Claims to Territory Between Japan and Korea in International Law.* Bloomington, IN: Xlibris, 2014.

Klinck, Heino. "Japan's Defense Priorities and Implications for the U.S.-Japan Alliance." Center for Strategic and International Studies, June 23, 2023, www.csis.org > analysis > japan-defense…

Koseki, Shoichi. *The Birth of Japan's Postwar Constitution.* Edited and translated by Ray A. Moore. Boulder, CO: Westview Press, 1997.

Large, Stephen S. *Emperor Hirohito and Showa Japan: A Political Biography.* New York: Routledge, 1992.

Lee, Seokwoo, ed. *Encyclopedia of Ocean Law and Policy in Asia-Pacific.* Boston: Brill/Nijhoff, 2023.

Liff, Adam P. and Jeffrey W. Hornung. "Japan's New Security Policies: A Long Road to Full Implementation." Rand Corporation, March 27, 2023, www.rand.org > … > Blog.

Lind, Jennifer. *Sorry States: Apologies in International Politics.* Ithaca, NY: Cornell University Press, 2008.

MacArthur, Douglas. *Reminiscences.* New York: McGraw-Hill, 1964.

Maki, John M. *Court and Constitution in Japan: Selected Supreme Court Decisions,* 1948-60. Seattle: University of Washington Press, 1964.

Maki, John M. "The Documents of Japan's Commission on the Constitution." *Journal of Asian Studies* 24 (1965): 475-89.

Maki, John M. trans. and ed. *Japan's Commission on the Constitution: The Final Report.* Seattle: University of Washington Press, 1980.

McNelly, Theodore H. "'Induced Revolution': The Policy and Process of Constitutional Reform in Occupied Japan." In Ward and Sakamoto, *Democratizing Japan,* 79-110.

McNelly, Theodore H. *The Origins of Japan's Democratic Constitution.* Lanham, MD: University Press of America, 2000.

McNelly, Theodore H., ed. *Sources in Modern East Asian History and Politics.* New York: Appleton-Century-Crofts, 1967.

Midford, Paul. *Rethinking Japanese Public Opinion and Security: From Pacifism to Realism?* Stanford: Stanford University Press, 2011.

Miller, J. Berkshire. "The ICJ and the Dokdo/Takeshima Dispute," *The Diplomat* (May 13, 2014), https//thediplomat.com > authors.

Moore, Ray A. and Donald L. Robinson. *Partners for Democracy: Crafting the New Japanese State Under MacArthur.* New York: Oxford University Press, 2002.

Nagai, Yonosuke and Akira Iriye, eds. *The Origins of the Cold War in Asia.* New York: Columbia University Press, 1977.

National Archives, Diplomatic Section. Notter Files, Box 57, 63, 65, 142.

National Diet Library (*Kokuritsu kokkai toshokan*). part1. sec. 2, https://www.ndl.go.jp > shiryo.

Norris, Robert S., William M. Arkin, and William Burr. "Where They Were, How Much Did Japan Know?" *The Bulletin of the Atomic Scientists*: 56, no. 1 (January-February 2000).

O'Hanlon, Michael E. *The Senkaku Paradox: Risking Great Power War Over Small Stakes.* Washington, DC: Brookings Institution Press, 2019.

Orr, James J. *The Victim as Hero: Ideologies of Peace and National Identity in Postwar Japan.* Honolulu: University of Hawai'i Press, 2001.

Ota, Masahide. "The U.S. Occupation of Okinawa and Postwar Reforms in Japan Proper." In Ward and Sakamoto, *Democratizing Japan,* 283-304.

Sasaki, Tomoyuki. "The Constitution Must Be Defended: Thoughts on the Constitution's Role in Japan's Postwar Democracy," *The Asia-Pacific Journal: Japan Focus* 16, issue 20, no. 3 (October 15, 2018).

Sasaki, Tomoyuki. "Whose Peace? Anti-Military Litigation and the Right to Live in Peace in Postwar Japan," *The Asia-Pacific Journal: Japan Focus* 10, issue 29, no. 1 (July 9, 2012), https://apjjf.org > - Tomoyuki Sasaki.

Sato, Tatsuo. "The Origin and Development of the Draft Constitution of Japan," *Contemporary Japan* 24, nos. 4-6 (1956): 175-87, and 24, nos. 7-9 (1956): 371-87.

Sato, Yoichiro and Astha Chadha. "Understanding the Senkaku/Diaoyu Islands Dispute: Diplomatic, Legal, and Strategic Contexts." E-International Relations, https://www.e-ir.info > 2022/06/23.

Scalapino, Robert A. and Junnosuke Masumi. *Parties and Politics in Contemporary Japan.* Berkeley: University of California Press, 1962.

Smith, Sheila A. "How Japan is Doubling Down on Its Military Power." Council on Foreign Relations, December 20, 2022, www.cfr.org > article > how. japan.doubl...

Smith, Sheila A. *Intimate Rivals: Japanese Domestic Politics and a Rising China.* New York: Columbia University Press, 2015.

Smith, Sheila A. *Japan Rearmed: The Politics of Military Power.* Cambridge, MA: Harvard University Press, 2019.

Sodei, Rinjiro. *Dear General MacArthur: Letters from the Japanese during the American Occupation.* Lanham, MD: Rowan & Littlefield, 2001.

Sugita, Yoneyuki. "The Yoshida Doctrine as a Myth," *The Japanese Journal of American Studies,* no. 27 (2016): 123-43.

Supreme Commander for the Allied Powers, Government Section. *Political Reorientation of Japan, September 1945 to September 1948.* 2 vols. Washington, DC: Government Printing Office, 1949.

Takayanagi, Kenzo. "Some Reminiscences of Japan's Commission on the Constitution." In Henderson, *The Constitution of Japan,* 71-88.

Takemae, Eiji. *The Allied Occupation of Japan.* Translated by Robert Ricketts and Sebastian Swann. New York: Continuum International Publishing Group, 2002.

Tokuchi, Hideshi. "Japan's New National Security Strategy and Contribution to a Networked Regional Security Architecture." Center for Strategic and International Studies, June 23, 2023, www.csis.org > analysis > japans-new-nat...

Tsuji, Kiyoaki, ed. *Shiryo—sengo nijunenshi.* Tokyo: Nihon hyoronsha, 1966, 1:661.

United Nations Convention on the Law of the Sea, Part 5: Exclusive Economic Zone, Article 60.

United Nations Convention on the Law of the Sea, Part 12: Protection and Preservation of the Marine Environment, Section 1: General Provisions, Article 192.

United Nations Treaty Collection. "Treaty of Peace with Japan. Signed at San Francisco, on 8 September 1951." *Treaty Series* 48, 50, 1952, https://treaties.un.org > unts.

Ward, Robert E. "The Commission on the Constitution and Prospects for Constitutional Change in Japan." *Journal of Asian Studies* 24 (1965): 401-29.

Ward, Robert E. and Yoshikazu Sakamoto, eds. *Democratizing Japan: The Allied Occupation.* Honolulu: University of Hawai'i Press, 1987.

Ward, Robert E. "Presurrender Planning: Treatment of the Emperor and Constitutional Change." In Ward and Sakamoto, *Democratizing Japan,* 1-45.

Weinstein, Martin E. *Japan's Postwar Defense Policy, 1947-1968.* New York: Columbia University Press, 1971.

Yanagihashi, Minoru. "The Territorial Questions in East Asia and San Francisco Peace Treaty: Historical Perspective." Paper presented at the Association for Asian Studies 2011 Annual Conference, Honolulu, April 2011.

Yoshida, Shigeru. *The Yoshida Memoirs: The Story of Japan in Crisis.* Translated by Kenichi Yoshida. Boston: Houghton Mifflin, 1962.

Yuan, Jingdong. "Japan's New Military Policies: Origins and Implications." Stockholm International Peace Research Institute, February 2, 2023, https://www.sipri. org > about > bios.

Zakowski, Karol. "Kochikai of the Japanese Liberal Democratic Party and Its Evolution After the Cold War." *The Korean Journal of International Studies* 9, no. 2 (December 2011): 179-205.

www.ingramcontent.com/pod-product-compliance
Lightning Source LLC
Chambersburg PA
CBHW040854210326
41597CB00029B/4847